THE BOOK YOU
READ TO TEACH
YOUR CHILDREN

THE BOOK YOU READ TO TEACH YOUR CHILDREN

Eight Ways to Keep Learning at Home Fun

Katie Tollitt

S

First published in 2020 by Orion Spring,
an imprint of The Orion Publishing Group Ltd
Carmelite House, 50 Victoria Embankment,
London EC4Y ODZ

An Hachette UK company

1 3 5 7 9 10 8 6 4 2

A CIP catalogue record for this book is
available from the British Library.

ISBN (Hardback): 978 1 398 701076
ISBN (eBook): 978 1 398 701083

Typeset by Born Group
Printed in Great Britain by Clays Ltd, Elcograf S.p.A.

www.orionbooks.co.uk

'Education is not the filling of a pail, but the lighting of a fire'

Plutarch

Contents

Introduction

If you are reading this book, it's likely you are a parent interested in becoming more involved in your child or children's education at home.* Understandably this can feel like a daunting prospect – after all, you already have one (incredibly important) relationship with your child, and being a teacher is an entirely separate full-time job which requires training and many years of experience to fully develop its skills. Furthermore, the first day of school is often celebrated as a milestone for your child; it's the day on which they begin to step out into the world. Many parents may consider school to be the main place for a child to develop their social, emotional and academic skills, and the idea of trying to *do* school at home feels pretty much impossible. I want to reassure you that these

---

* Throughout the book I will use the terms 'parent' and 'child', though I know there are differently shaped families in which siblings, uncles, grandparents and many other sorts of carers play the role of parent. Likewise, there is a whole other book to be written on children that require extra support at school, as well as their specific and unique learning needs. Taking that into consideration, I hope that the broad principles of this book will be applicable to anyone looking to facilitate the learning of a child at home.

feelings are perfectly natural and that you are not alone.

As I sit writing this in April 2020, around the world millions of parents are facing up to being suddenly thrust into the role of teacher as well as parent and, if social media is anything to go by, finding this challenging and undeniably a little stressful. If any of the below feels familiar:

'I can't get them to concentrate without bribes!'

'We lasted ten minutes, and now she's refusing to do anything.'

'*Frozen 2* counts as English *and* science, right?'

. . . then perhaps this book may be able to provide ideas and some support for you. I don't want to promise that I can remove the stress entirely. As parents and teachers, we all agree that the best way to prepare our children for success as adults is to pass on a love of learning at a young age. We may worry that by trying to help our children, we are actually hindering the process of self-discovery (this is an important balance teachers try to find in the classroom each day, too). I am writing this book because I believe there are some key principles that will help parents as they support their child's education at home, minimise avoidable conflict, keep learning fun and ultimately prevent parents from worrying about finding a healthy work–life balance for their family. You are most likely going to be teaching in among a great many other things, unable to give the amount of time and focus teachers can provide in a school environment. In this context, I believe it's even more important to try and make the most of the time you are able to spend, and for everyone to feel as good as they can about the process.

My own background as a primary school teacher has equipped me with many different skills which inform this book. I trained and taught as part of the British education system before moving to Hong Kong to work internationally, and I have been constantly on the lookout for ways to improve my own knowledge and skill set. This book will allow me to share my passion for teaching and learning, in addition to offering my experience of supporting parents in a range of different learning contexts. I certainly don't claim to be the world's foremost expert on teaching, but I dedicate a great deal of my time to supporting people who have an interest in education and, through my work online, communicating with teachers as they start out on their journey. I therefore feel I've got a good grasp of what can flummox someone as they begin teaching.

This book is likely to be most useful to parents of primary school children. It may be even more useful for parents of younger primary children, who will probably be bringing work home for the first time, and who do not have home learning routines set up yet. While children are developing initial skills, such as letter formation and early number work, it can be especially difficult to establish a schedule that feels fair, achievable and manageable. What we want is to find a healthy balance between guided work and skills gained more independently, and to encourage and build a love for learning.

Throughout the book I want you to keep in mind these seven fundamental ideas:

1. Teaching can be very difficult – finding it hard doesn't mean either you or your child is doing anything wrong. As a computer programmer would say, it's a feature, not a bug.

2. Children's brains are not just smaller adult brains – the way they approach learning, take in information and retain it, as well as how long they can concentrate on a task is very different. If you judge them by adult criteria, they will fail almost every time. If you are aware of this, then you can try to avoid doing so.

3. Children's learning is almost never a neat forward progression – moments of plateau and a couple of steps backwards are a natural and essential part of learning. The struggle is real!

4. Every child is different – just because you, or your niece or nephew could do something by a certain age, or enjoy something in particular, doesn't mean that your child should, too. Respect what makes your child unique.

5. Children are incredibly adaptable – they're not going to permanently 'fall behind', and may even learn a whole new set of skills at home.

6. You may find the process stressful, but the fact that you care deeply means you'll most likely find a way to make it work.

7. When everything clicks, teaching a new skill can be incredibly rewarding. Learning more about your child through an academic lens may help you get to know each other in a new and deeply fulfilling way.

While I have included some examples for practical exercises and project ideas, this book is far more about the underlying fundamentals of how we can approach learning. When I speak to parents, I often find that their frustration stems from not having anything to measure their child against. As adults, though we have all been through this stage of early development, for most of us it was such a long time ago we can barely remember the process. It is hard for us to comprehend what's going on inside our child's mind during this stage of their learning. Taking this into consideration, it is even more important that we teach our children with an open mind.

Teachers have a range of ways in which we gather information about the ability of a child, having guided many children through this stage of their learning. As a parent at home with your child, it's likely that you'll be comparing your child to the (probably fictional) versions of children you hear about on the grapevine, or those carefully curated versions you see online. There may be children that immediately sit quietly and are utterly focused on their workbooks for hours at a time, but I promise you the vast majority of them do not, or at least, it's a long road to get there. Nothing demotivates as efficiently as setting unrealistic targets which are missed, and nothing encourages as much as breaking things into tiny steps and taking them alongside your child.

One of the things you may also have to get past is your own relationship with learning. If you didn't particularly enjoy school, then you're going to have to try not to let this impact how your child feels about it at home. Conversely, if you have positive associations with school, it can be frustrating if your child doesn't seem to share that passion. You may be able to relate to the idea that a family member is not always the best person to learn a new skill from; there is a reason why we often respond more professionally and sensibly when a lesson is taught by someone with whom we have less of an emotional connection. That's where I hope some of the techniques in this book – techniques for taking a moment, stepping back and communicating with one another – will be useful in developing positive relationships.

Since every child is different, I want to try and promote a practical approach that will help you understand your child's learning style and unique set of needs. I am not going to tell you which workbook for which subject you should be teaching at half past ten on a Tuesday – in fact, as you'll see, I think that integrating core subjects such as English, Mathematics and Science into project-based work will be far more stimulating for you and your child.

Ideally, this book will help you develop a flexible learning environment driven by your child's ideas. I hope it will be a book you can read when preparing for remote learning, before you approach the coming week, or however works best for you as a parent. I hope, too, that it will be a motivating resource that will inspire you to create fun and exciting learning opportunities alongside your child.

Part I

—

Preparation

I.

When is a classroom not a classroom?

Building an effective learning environment

You've bought all of the workbooks online. You've colour-coded your comprehensive timetable for a whole day of learning (and proudly posted it online). It's 9 a.m. – time to get teaching!

Hang on.

While it might be tempting to jump head first into structured academic learning, before you do that it's important to create a positive learning environment for you and your child. In the same way that you need time to prepare, they will also need to adjust to the new expectations and physical surroundings. Teachers work hard to make sure that their classrooms are bright, inviting and organised (at least for the start of the year!). You are not going to be expected to replicate your child's classroom exactly, so you don't need to feel guilty for making do with what you have available. Take time to set up a positive workspace, and allow yourself to enjoy the design process. Your child will know if they are being rushed, and will appreciate being given the chance to make creative decisions. If you are fortunate enough to have a quiet space away from the main living area, this can work well as a way of signifying that when you enter that area of the house, you are entering the learning environment. Don't worry if you don't have space to do that; classrooms are often crowded places too, and children normally adapt well to the space they have available to them.

GET THEM INVOLVED

First, consider asking your child what they like most about their classroom at school. A simple, open-ended question such as '**What do you like most about how your classroom looks?**' should do the trick. Take notes from their response, considering the little details that mean a lot to them. If they are stuck for an answer, guide them by suggestion, using questions such as:

'**What do you first notice when you enter the room?**'

Or even:

'**What is your favourite thing to look at when you are in the classroom?**'

Perhaps they like the fairy lights, reading corner cushions and plush classroom mascot that appears to greet them each morning as they walk through the door. Although it might not be possible to recreate every detail, it might make for a nice activity that can be shared with your child while working to set up a comfortable learning environment. You might notice that I am trying to avoid calling it a classroom; most teachers believe learning can take place in all sorts of different environments, rather than just the confines of a traditional classroom. You want to make sure your child knows that you are not trying to exactly replicate something, but that you are working together to create something new.

SETTING UP

If you're someone who can work perfectly well with a cluttered desk, don't assume this style will also work for your child. Likewise, if you order your desk with zen-like precision, don't stop them from personalising their surroundings with decoration and objects that are theirs. Give them the opportunity to arrange their workspace; signs, posters and decoration might mean a lot to them aesthetically, so don't rush to get past this stage in order to access the more academic 'work'. If you find that they are enthused by the idea of making the space theirs, then designing it on paper first before making it happen in real life can be a really exciting activity to do together.

Teachers love to give students the opportunity to bring their creations to life as often as we are able. As teachers, we are always looking for ways to incorporate our core subjects into larger long-term projects. In this way, rather than doing twenty minutes of 'maths' and twenty minutes of 'English', we might measure the space for a poster, write down the measurements, design the poster, pick which words will go on it and practise our writing and shapes. We want our children to understand that learning is an important part of our lives, an active process in which any opportunity could present the chance to learn something new.

Preparing for project-based learning may also play an important role in the early set-up stages of learning from home, one which will establish important fundamentals. Communicate with your child as part of this process; use open-ended questions such as:

'What sort of materials do you think we might need to keep close by as we start our home learning?'

'What might we need to collect later on, for our future projects?'

Questions like this will show that your initial set-up is subject to change and that your environment will grow and adapt to suit their needs. Depending on your child's personality, you might find they make some interesting requests regarding what they are allowed to bring with them to a workspace. In the past I have worked alongside younger children who have been keen to bring a favourite toy (or indeed, a number of toys) along to a lesson. Instead of telling them this is an automatic no, ask them what their reason for choosing this toy or object might be. You could even add it into your daily routine and suggest they choose a small, unobtrusive toy to bring along each day. Younger children can always explain their ideas to their chosen toy, or it could be used as an example when describing or modelling the use of speech. Younger children sometimes prefer to share or whisper ideas to toys or even animals when given the chance, and for some children it may provide an element of comfort. If something appears to be important to your child, communication can help you to incorporate it within your home learning approach rather than ruling it out completely.

Reflecting on their own school experiences, parents may think that a teacher needs to fulfil a strict disciplinarian role (consider how teachers are often portrayed on television and in film as fierce, dominant forces!). In reality, in a modern school, teachers will very rarely rely solely on their authority to justify why a child should do what they say. There have to be boundaries, consequences and agreed rules of conduct, but they are part of a conversation in which puzzling through together why that is the case is part of the learning, rather than handing rules down from on high.

2.

Effective communication

Your child's unique learning style

The first thing to keep in mind is that all children are different. As a teacher, I very rarely set the exact same challenge to each student in the same way. That's because we now understand that children learn in different ways – we sometimes refer to that as a 'learning style'. Some children respond positively to visuals such as images, videos and flash cards, while others may prefer audio instructions or physical, tactile apparatus.

Three examples of learning styles that are used within the primary classroom are based around a formalised system called the 'VAK' learning styles*. Teachers will often refer to this when resourcing lessons, as it can be

---

* There is ongoing discussion among teachers about how useful this model is. In the past it has been taught that a student is of a certain type which is now less commonly accepted. I find it most useful as a shorthand for remembering to vary your approach, stay flexible and remember that learning presents in all sorts of different ways.

useful for children to be given work that incorporates a blend of each learning style.

VISUAL

V stands for visual learning. Visual learners will benefit from thinking about how information is displayed with illustrations, photographs and videos. It may be really useful for your child to see your facial expression and body language when you are talking them through a set of instructions. For older visual learners, encouraging them to take notes can work really well, as this visual process will help them to consolidate their ideas. These learners may respond well to a visual timetable full of images and colours that represent different activities or parts of the day.

AUDITORY

A stands for auditory learning. Auditory learners are more likely to respond to lessons that focus on listening and discussion, rather than information written down. They may be picking up a lot of information through the way something is being said – the pitch and tone of a voice, the speed of speech and even through music or connecting with sound effects. You could try recording your lessons, allowing them to listen to them again if they want to. Try to read back over instructions out loud with a couple of different phrasings to check they've been fully understood, before asking your child to explain them to you. Audiobooks may work well when supporting this learning style, as it might help your child to visualise a story or character through audio description rather than using images. Auditory learners may also make connections between songs and events, which might mean they respond well to having music played in the background of their lessons.

KINAESTHETIC

K stands for kinaesthetic learning, or what's sometimes referred to as physical learning. These learners benefit from physical activities, often choosing to explore using touch, preferring to handle items in order to gather information. They may find it harder to sit down and listen to long lessons, or read extended paragraphs of instruction. Instead, consider ways in which you can bring a physical element to your lessons, including actions, gestures and items that can be held. Rather than asking your child to draw five shapes, consider asking them to make a tower that is five cubes high. If you are worried about your child insisting on holding on to items while you are working with them, for example playing with a pen lid or bouncing an eraser, try asking them a question that relates to the work. If they are able to answer the question, try not to worry about the item causing a distraction. It might actually be helping them to stay focused! In the past I have given my students plasticine to make shapes with, paper to shred and even squishy toys to hold. If it becomes too distracting and the child cannot engage with the learning, I know to remove the item, but if they are still able to connect, it might be supporting their kinaesthetic learning style.

Ultimately it can be useful to think about which learning style your child might favour; however, in practice you will find that most children need a mixture of different learning styles. Their preferred way of learning may change depending on the lesson being taught, or may even move from one style to another as they grow and try out new ways in which to learn. It's useful to keep these learning styles in mind, but you will almost certainly find that a balance of all three works best.

Children rarely respond to a challenge in exactly the same way, so consider carefully how you're asking them to fulfil a task and the resources that may need to be provided alongside it. The ideal dynamic is that you're asking a child to do something because you've helped them to understand why it matters, not that you're telling them to do something because they have to do what you say.

Before you jump into any sort of work, it's worth spending time figuring out how your child prefers to learn. Rather than enforcing an expectation of how the learning will take place from an initial lesson, open up a discussion with your child. Consider using open-ended questions such as:

'**What sort of activities do you enjoy in school?**'

Answers such as '**My teacher makes us laugh, he has a funny puppet that talks to us**' may indicate that your child enjoys engaging through audio, and that they like to share their thoughts through imaginative play.

If they respond with something more logical, such as '**We do fun puzzles when it's maths time!**' it is possible that your child enjoys numerical, problem-solving challenges.

Take notes together and use this first 'lesson' to gather as much information as you can about your child. Your child's class teacher most likely spent the first couple of weeks communicating with your child, making careful notes about their likes, dislikes and interests. Most children are a blend of different learning styles in different contexts. This is an opportunity to learn alongside them: what do they enjoy doing? What sort of task do they get distracted by, and what do they become immersed in? Rather than thinking that children work best when sitting quietly at a table, see what happens if you get active, involve a musical instrument or get them building and creating.

WHY IS THIS IMPORTANT?

This process of preparation can be an ideal opportunity to talk about why you're going to be learning. Asking an open-ended question such as '**How do you know if you have done a good job with your work?**' may help you to figure out your child's personal values and how they view their own contribution to learning. Their response might provoke an interesting discussion, as well as help you to understand the classroom management systems your child has been exposed to.

A reply such as '**Well, the teacher will tick it if it is correct**' will suggest that they have an understanding of a definitive right or wrong answer.

A response such as '**My teacher will smile and say well done!**' perhaps suggests that they have more of an emotional connection to their academic work, and that they see success as something to be shared. Some children thrive off external praise, for example seeing their work on display or sharing it with others, whereas other children may be self-motivated by their own perception of their work, and may be able to give a specific example of why they like it.

You're in this together

You'll possibly be familiar with the idea of shared goals in a professional context. When a group of adults are working together on a project, or alongside one another within a company, they will create a project agreement in which all members of the party will share their strategies for effective communication. This appears to be used to help minimise inevitable disagreements and to maximise effective work time. Consider how this strategy might be effective when cultivating a positive work environment for your child; it's a respectful way of setting boundaries that may help to keep everyone on track.

For this task, I suggest opening a discussion by asking your child, '**Why is learning important?**' This is something worth discussing with them right at the start. School is generally accepted as an environment where the value of learning is communicated in many different ways both explicitly and more subtly. The very act of them being taken there, and the routine of all the different children arriving together communicates that what happens there is important. We spend a lot of time as teachers explaining how their learning experiences are all interconnected, often choosing to symbolise this importance through a strategy of reward points, putting work up on the walls or embarking on long-term projects, so we are constantly reinforcing that sense of collective school and class identity through shared goals and purpose. Feedback and reflection is used continuously to highlight the value of learning as part of the whole school community. This is going to need to be approached differently at home, where much of the dynamic will be different. Consider ways to make it clear right at the beginning that the things you will be doing have a purpose and that you will be going through it together.

Minimising problems

As parents, you know that a conflict can appear as if from nowhere, even when everything seems to be running smoothly. Of course, you won't want to start off by imagining the worst, but time spent up front agreeing on how to communicate when things aren't going well is key.

Try asking, **'How will I know if you need a break from this – what signals will you give me?'**

As well as: **'If we have a disagreement, what will be best for us to do?'**

A child may need support in figuring out the answer to such meaningful questions, but hopefully they will be able to articulate strategies such as:

'I prefer to have some time to myself when I need to reflect.'

Or, **'Sometimes I get frustrated when I work for too long. Playing with my toys or listening to my favourite song helps me calm down.'** They may be unable to verbalise this with such accuracy, but a discussion will allow you to help them discover strategies that may be useful to them now and in the future, too.

Once you've completed this discussion, it could be helpful to look over any notes you have made alongside your child in order to create an agreement. Be sure to take their words, notions and input into consideration. Your agreement can be something you write together, design and make into a document or poster that you can include in your routine by referring to it at the beginning and end of each day.

Example learning agreement

1. I learn best when my dad shows me an example first.

2. I like activities that include pictures and videos best.

3. When I need a break, I will tell you.

4. If I feel frustrated, I like to listen to a calm song.

5. I know that even if we disagree, my mum is trying her best to support me.

6. I understand that this type of learning will not be exactly the same as school.

7. When I enjoy a challenge, I will tell you.

8. You can leave me to work independently after we discuss the task together first.

9. I know that this is a new challenge for my dad too.

10. If I have an idea for a project, I will write it in my notepad.

Consider making a learning agreement for yourself as well as one for your child. This will show your child that you are equally enthused and keen to stay on track, and that these agreements have a purpose. A shared sense of accountability and mutual respect will start things off strongly.

Understanding verbal and non-verbal signals

During parent–teacher conferences, I am often told by parents that they are confused as to why their children respond so differently to tasks in the classroom to tasks they are asked to do at home. I believe many teachers would agree that the classroom environment provides a safe place where children are provided with structure, routine and everything they need to carry out most tasks. Although children often have access to technology and toys when at home, it is unlikely their home environment will mimic that of the classroom. Considering this, it is to be expected that children will have a harder time expressing their wants, needs and requirements when exposed to a different work environment.

Children may say they are hungry, tired or need a break when truthfully they are struggling with a work task. This is something a lot of children will try in the classroom when they first join a new class: children will say they need a toilet break in order to avoid something that is presenting a challenge to them. For the teacher, there are methods that are often used to help identify when a child is asking for a break or purposefully avoiding a task. Asking a child to complete a paragraph or set of questions before going for a snack or toilet break is perfectly acceptable and will help to indicate whether or not the student is looking for an excuse.

Communication through questions such as **'Do you need a break, or is the work confusing you?'** may help to break down the barriers that a child has built in order to avoid the task at hand. Be honest with your children; I often use phrases such as:

'I know this part is difficult. I understand it would be easier to walk away and play on your iPad, however, I think it is important that we try to solve the problem together first. Think how great you will feel once we manage to figure this out together!'

Being transparent and honest with children is often the most effective tool we have. Children seem to be very aware of bribes for their own sake and may respond better to reasoning. The trick is to empower children, allowing them to take ownership of their academic achievements.

Reward and reflection

If your child's school follows a structured behaviour policy, I would suggest that using the policy within a home learning environment might not be the best idea. Of course you are welcome to try, but based on my own experience it can be difficult for anyone to replicate the systems that have been installed by a classroom teacher.

When I mentor trainee teachers, I often encourage them to develop a system for managing behaviour that is personal to them, taking inspiration from the systems adopted by the school. People may have varied opinions on this, but I do think it would be better to consider a system of your own, rather than applying something that your child's teacher uses within the classroom. In addition to this, your child's teachers have probably received an abundance of training specifically looking at positive and negative forms of classroom management. It's a lot to try and learn if you are suddenly faced with the task of generating a system of your own. Work with what works best for you and your family, as this will surely be different to how systems look inside the classroom.

As an example, the class teacher might use a coloured traffic light system, where students are expected to move their name to a different colour depending on the behaviour choices they have made on a particular day. Although this might be effective in the classroom, it would be tricky to implement within your home; the classroom teacher may have time designated for reflection, as well as a reward system that has been developed alongside their students. If you feel as though you might want to introduce some sort of reward or behaviour management system within your home, consider asking your child about how this is arranged in their classroom before creating your own variation. As always, it can be useful to encourage your child to reflect with you on the decision they have made, though perhaps not choosing to do this when they are already angry, upset or frustrated. I would also highly recommend using an abundance of positive behaviour management strategies, being sure to notice the small actions your child makes throughout the day that help them to stay on track. They may be craving the structure and expectations they are used to from their classroom, so ask for their input when considering implementing this at home.

What have we learnt?

During parent–teacher conferences, I often hear similar statements being made about students. Parents will tell me: '**I ask her about what she has done at school and she never wants to tell me, why is that?**' It's possible that we sometimes give our students questions they find difficult to answer, due to the potential response being vast and hard to put into words. It's often more effective to break up conversations into questions that are easier to process. An example might be:

'**I remember you have art class on a Tuesday. Did you learn any new skills in your art lesson today?**'

Or, '**Did you notice anyone being kind to someone else in class today?**'

This same manageable, open-ended questioning approach can be applied to home learning challenges too. If you ask children, '**Do you know this addition method?**' They will most likely respond with 'yes'. Consider ways in which you can open your question, such as,

'Can you explain the first part of this method to me?'

Better still, 'If we were teaching this method to someone who had not used it before, what might we say to them?'

This is where your plush toy friend from Chapter 1 may come in handy; children appear to enjoy teaching their understanding to someone, or even some*thing*, who appears to be younger or less knowledgeable than they are. In the classroom, I always use this to my advantage and allow the children plenty of time to present their findings to their peers. Sometimes I might even pair up my class with a younger group in order to allow my students the opportunity to share their exciting new knowledge with an audience. It could be useful to build in a part of the day where you ask your child to teach what they've learnt to their toy. Or perhaps you could agree with another parent that your children could video-call and explain to each other what they've done that day.

3.

Scheduling and organisation of assignments

Creating a timetable and setting up routines

You've designed your learning environment together, and created the framework for why learning is important and how you'll respect one another. Now it's time to think about a timetable.

Regardless of their age or their academic ability, my students seem always to have an innate natural ability when it comes to memorising a timetable. Usually they are quicker than I am when remembering what lesson is coming up, especially if it's a lesson they particularly look forward to. Although this is developed over many initial weeks of practising a repeated routine, I am constantly impressed by how well children adapt to the timetable of the primary classroom. If I ever want something important to be remembered for me, my students will act as little memo pads, chirping up to let me know that I am supposed to drop the laptop trolley key back to the technology lab by the end of the day.

Never underestimate their ability to synchronise with a routine; at least give them the opportunity to show they can do this, rather than take control, which I know can be tempting.

Creating a timetable will require patience, revision and positive, open communication with your child. There are lots of excellent examples of home learning timetables available online at the moment which you could reference when working to build one that suits you. Consider looking at the timetable your child has been using at school to find a way to structure your own. Open-ended questioning might not work as well with your child, here; it might be easier to ask more direct questions in order to build a visual picture of their day.

'**What is the first thing you do when you go into your classroom?**'

To which you may receive a reply such as '**I sign in by moving my picture onto the class rainbow. Then I say hello to Ms Worringham.**'

'**Ah, I see. And do you think we need to sign in to our home learning sessions, too?**'

Already you have established a small, simple part of your daily routine. Your child would appreciate something visual to symbolise that the focused learning time has begun. Perhaps they also enjoy starting their day with a greeting or an informal conversation. My students love to come and share little anecdotes about their lives with me first thing in the morning, and when I have some free time available, my favourite thing to do is have a conversation with them that doesn't need to link to our learning in any way. This is when we bond and I learn about their families, pets and friends.

You may want to draw out a template for your time-table on paper, or print out an empty example you've found online. Having several different examples ready to present to your child will avoid the shoulder shrug that may be the response when you ask your child to create one from scratch. Consider collecting three examples and bringing them to your newly created learning environment at the start of the day. Discuss what you like and dislike about each template, giving reasons to support your thoughts. Use a pencil to make draft notes about where each subject will go, reinforcing through dialogue that the structure can change on reflection at the end of the week. Although it's necessary to stick to a timetable, as adults we know that some things may need to be adjusted over time in order to stay relevant and useful.

When incorporating academic subjects into your time-table, try to keep your child engaged with shorter bursts of learning, especially when balancing this alongside independent activities. You might want to build up by starting out with no more than ten or fifteen minutes of focused learning at a time, remembering that certain tasks will capture your child's attention more than others. Different activities will appeal to different children. Building-block construction may keep a child's attention for over an hour, whereas drawing a picture may hold limited interest for them. As a guideline, I always try to schedule subjects that require more reasoning and focus earlier in the morning and save my enquiry-based, project-style learning for the afternoon, when it is usually harder for students to retain concentration. Some children might take longer to engage, so this approach may differ for you and your child; another reason why reflecting on your timetable at the end of each week is so valuable. If your child becomes engrossed with a task such as story-writing or a science project, there is no harm in rearranging some activities or moving them to a slot later in the week. Teachers do this all the time in class, depending on how their students respond to a given task. Structure is important, but it should be flexible structure. There is nothing worse than being forced to bring an activity to an end when your students are finally settling into it!

You're not on your own – but don't be afraid to find your own solutions

As I write this in the spring of 2020, many parents are supporting their children's learning at home while on lockdown. Unprecedented times have called for schools to act using their initiative, providing remote support for students despite not having had adequate time to prepare for such an event. It is essential not to focus on what your child may be missing out on, as this may well be out of your control, but rather to look at the skills they may gain as a result of following this new style of learning. Your child's teacher will most likely be providing lessons, resources and a string of continually changing expectations for you to unpick, understand and respond to each day. Each school will have a different approach to this, as well as different ways of providing feedback to their students.

If a task is presented to you which requires use of an unfamiliar website, be sure to check in with your child first: you could be spending valuable time teaching yourself to use something that perhaps your child could teach you. Reinforcing knowledge through instruction is a method we always try to encourage as teachers. Allow your child to show you how to use something, especially if they have a lot of experience of using it in class. A dialogue to check this might look like the following:

'**Have you used this website before in class? How does it work?**'

Hoping for a response such as: '**We use this website to answer questions about books. It's like a quiz, but online.**'

Further encourage your child to share by asking, '**Can you show me how this works? Can you show me how you use this in class?**'

You might need to build on your knowledge through some research of your own, but it's nice to allow your child to introduce it to you if they are able, especially as each school may be using a website in its own unique way. Don't worry if you feel overwhelmed by all of this information up front. The most important thing is to find a system that works for you and your child. You can start to join that up with the school's structures later on, once you've got into a routine of learning at home.

Balancing independent learning with providing support

Consider making space in your timetable at the start of the day for a set of simple questions that will help your child to focus. If your child is younger, I often recommend having them use the fingers on their hand to express how they feel about something. For example, I might say: **'Use your hand to show me how confident you feel about trying some new punctuation in our sentences today.'** Five fingers may represent confidence, knowledge and independence, whereas fewer than three may symbolise that this is something your child doesn't yet fully understand, or is less motivated to complete.

Although children may prefer to complete work with you sitting by their side, it's important to leave space in the timetable for them to work independently on tasks. If your child is older, resources such as dictionaries, iPads (you may wish to monitor this) and reference books may be useful to have close by; encourage your child to utilise the resources around them before turning to you for a solution. Even with younger children, leaving them to puzzle through something for a while on their own can be a really valuable part of learning. I generally implement an 'ask three before me' rule in the classroom, promoting peer-to-peer support among my students. As your child may be completing the work by themselves, you could encourage a 'try three resources before asking me' rule, inviting them to look back over the questions asked as well as use the resources around them before reaching out for support. Asking them, **'What do you think you might need to complete this task?'** before setting them off may be useful; you can write the key items down on a list so they know where to find additional support.

4.

Acquiring and organising resources

Gathering the resources needed for effective home learning may, at first, feel like going on a scavenger hunt. You know that your child is going to need a range of different resources at their disposal, but you may struggle to create a list of requirements, especially when you're unsure what's usually available to groups of children in the primary classroom. When considering the resources you're going to need, I have a couple of 'non-negotiables' you may want to collect before you begin tackling the task at hand.

How is my child taught?

It could be useful for you to have copies of documents from your child's school. You may want to ask for a copy of the school's reading scheme, spelling scheme and phonics scheme. Although systems will vary depending on the way your child's school chooses to share this information, the school website may be a good place to go.

In addition, see if you can find or request a document stating which websites the school has set up for students, or has paid-for accounts with. It may be better to use websites that have been advised by the school, rather than hunting for new resources that will offer a similar service. It will help to get your children used to navigating resources that may be used regularly as they progress through the school. You might even find your child can access these websites independently, especially if they have been used before as part of their class-based lessons. We are always looking to promote independent learning!

Most schools will have something in place called a calculation policy: this is a document highlighting the way mathematical methods are taught in the school. For example, there are several different ways to multiply a number. As a child, you may have learnt to multiply in a different way to the one your child seems to have been taught. I understand how frustrating it must feel to be unable to support your child with their home learning without first working out for yourself the method they have been shown. Looking at addition, there may be a number of ways this is taught to your child, and it may change again depending on what year group they are in. You may already have received the school's calculation policy along with a handbook full of information at the start of your child's academic year. If you don't have this policy to hand, I recommend trying to obtain a copy by emailing your child's class teacher or looking on the school's website, where policies are often posted.

Having a copy of the calculation policy will help you to navigate the maths home learning tasks your child may be expected to complete without worrying that you are teaching them an unfamiliar method. On the other hand, we often encourage children to learn multiple methods, so if your child responds positively to the method you have introduced them to, allow them to embrace it alongside the method they may already have been taught at school.

The more knowledge you have of methods that are familiar to your child, the better chance you will have of reinforcing their understanding and helping them move on to embrace new academic challenges.

Finally, some schools will have a teaching and learning policy, and while a lot of the ideas won't necessarily blend seamlessly into the home learning environment, it may be worth looking over them while teaching from home. Hopefully this document will provide you with a basic idea of what sort of curriculum coverage would be expected of your child if they were in school. The school may also be able to give you a copy of their longer-term planning or curriculum overview.

Material resources

Although it is a good idea to gather resources as you progress through home learning projects, it may be useful to keep a kind of store cupboard of items located within easy reach of you and your child. I am aware that a lot of these items might not be readily available in your home, and that they might be difficult to track down externally, depending on the shops that are available to you. That being said, I hope this list will be useful for anyone who is starting to organise a bank of material resources:

1. Paper, in a range of different styles. Blank A4 is useful for making posters and for scrawling down project ideas. Lined paper, coloured sugar paper and larger flip chart-style paper may also be useful to have on hand.

2. Sticky notes can be used to record quick questions, targets and keywords. Keep a stack close by and don't be afraid to stick them around your learning environment, on mirrors or on the front of workbooks.

3. A glue stick is pretty self-explanatory, and is a useful resource to have on hand for design-based projects. There is a reason why we never seem to have enough glue sticks in the primary classroom – they get a lot of use.

4. A dry-wipe whiteboard is useful for recording quick calculations and letter formation. It also helps to minimise paper waste and clutter. If you don't have one available, a makeshift whiteboard can be made using a plastic wallet with a piece of paper inside. Keep it simple!

5. Construction materials such as building blocks or counters may be useful to have on hand: they can be used to show visual representations of calculations and patterns.

6. Recycling is a great way to minimise clutter and encourage children of all ages to take positive action. Labelling recycling bins, or simple cardboard boxes, is a great way to set up an organised learning environment. It's one of the first things I get my students to do at the start of a school year.

7. Pens, pencils, paintbrushes, paints, chalk and mark-making materials. They don't need to be organised with rainbow precision, but having a box full of these resources close by will help minimise the disruption of not having them handy during a moment of focus.

8. Having reading books close by, rather than in a different room, will give you the chance to pick up a quick read for them if you are ever in need of a break or moment of calm. If you have the space to create a small library, consider organising books into genres as an initial activity with your child.

9. A noticeboard or pinboard may be a nice way to keep relevant notes on display, as well as photographs, motivational posters and timetables. Allow your child to personalise this, taking ownership of arranging the memos and notices.

10. Easy-to-access technology devices should be located near a plug socket, with relevant cables, headphones, etc. close by. Although this might not be a requirement for each lesson, as a teacher I give my students the responsibility of ensuring their devices are charged and ready at the start of the school day.

More than a worksheet

Depending on the way your child's school chooses to structure their learning, your child may or may not have used worksheets as a way of collecting information. For your own sanity, I would suggest avoiding the temptation to print reams of pages out for your child to complete. In the classroom, most teachers will try to limit how many worksheets are given out to their students, preferring to concentrate on skills such as group work, practical activities and promoting questioning and research. If you have access to counters, cubes or even plastic figures, consider how much more effective it might be to allow your child to count or order these, rather than simply answering a row of questions given on a sheet. A whiteboard is a reusable way of recording their responses; you can always take a photograph of this to upload as evidence if it has been requested for their school portfolio.

As a teacher, if I'm using worksheets, I try to describe the tasks creatively, and in a way that is unique to each child. 'Patterns can be found all around us – in fact, I can see some from where I am sitting right now. Can you find a way to create a pattern with your group, and explain your reasoning to the rest of the class?' is arguably more effective than 'Circle the patterns on the sheet.' At the same time, do not feel guilty for choosing the second option. Teachers use a combination of both in order to stay balanced.

Research

First, your child is going to need a way to conduct their research. While we would like to think that a traditional method such as locating a keyword in a dictionary or hunting for a fact in an encyclopedia may be best, I can tell you that most teachers will probably be encouraging their students to use online search engines, not just because it is a faster way to gather information, but also because the information may be more up to date and relevant to the student. Plus, children seem to enjoy searching for information online. I don't think we should take that away from them; we should encourage them to work with technology, not always try to dissuade them from using it. That doesn't mean I think there is no place for a dictionary or an encyclopedia, or that we should avoid teaching children how to use them altogether – quite the opposite!

If we are to look at our home learning environments

practically, though, it makes perfect sense to have an online search engine set up and ready. Depending on what you have available, try to set up a screen so that your child can view it in front of them, closing any applications running in the background or recent online searches that may prove distracting to them. A laptop, or keyboard linked to a tablet, will enable your child to type; many online challenges that are set for students will require a typed response, even for younger students. In order to minimise potential disruptions, be sure to keep the device on charge, or a charger close by. If you are planning on using any online conferencing or video communication tools, you may also want to check that the camera and microphone are working correctly.

If your child is younger and therefore less able to access research tools independently, remember that research is a form of discovery. For a younger child, they might be researching by matching colours, ordering objects or making small discoveries. An example of this would be to give your child a range of different writing materials and encourage them to mimic letter shapes. Your child will hopefully realise that certain writing tools will make more effective marks on the page. Or, when asked to make connections between animals and their habitats, a child might be able to locate a page in a picture book where they have seen this kind of connection before. Research does not need to be limited to intentional discovery; a lot of what your child will find out will be accidental. Life is full of accidental discoveries!

Organising school email contacts, login details and links effectively

Your child will probably have a long list of codes, usernames and passwords that are necessary to unlock a range of different online applications, websites and even games. As a teacher, I am equally frustrated by how difficult it is to keep track of all of these codes. Sometimes websites may require unique combinations of words, numbers and symbols for each username. Certain usernames may have already been taken, forcing us to choose a password that is somewhat memorable; we try to make this as easy as possible for students, and us, to remember.

Find a notebook or an online document that will be easy to access for both you and your child and make a note of each login, even if this task proves time-consuming. I would also recommend making a list of important contacts, such as the email contact for your child's class teacher (if your school has chosen to provide this) as well as the school admin email, telephone number and a way of reaching the school's technology support team. Try to resist logging on to websites for your child; we always try to promote independence, even if it is frustrating to watch a child slowly type in each digit and search on the keyboard for the @ symbol. They need to practice this without our support. Only intervene if you sense they are truly struggling, or if the task of logging on is taking away too much learning time.

Find a balance between support and independence,

even with the smaller day-to-day tasks such as online admin. If your school is encouraging students to sign in each morning, try to make this a part of your routine and encourage your child to complete their attendance; offer plenty of praise when they remember by themselves in order to reinforce completion of this action. As a rule of thumb, if your child is able to do something independently, try to encourage this, no matter how small it may seem.

E-Safety

E-Safety, or Electronic Safety, is a term often used in discussing ways to keep students safe when using the internet or electronic devices. Most schools will have a policy set up with expectations that students and teachers will follow having embraced technology as part of the curriculum. If it's not already available on your school's website, you are within your rights to ask to look at the policy your child's school is using. As a teacher, I understand that allowing children access to the full features of the internet may cause you feelings of discomfort as a parent. We are all responsible when protecting our students from negative exposure online. If you search online for E-Safety, there are many different articles, blogs and documents highlighting steps you can take when preparing devices for children to use. I suggest doing some research and setting up the 'child friendly' version of video-browsing websites such as YouTube.

Although it may sound intrusive, I would also keep a close eye on the search history tab of your child's device; this way you can try to make sure they are not exposed to any online content that is not suitable for their age. I would even discuss this with your child, letting them know you are working hard to keep them safe. Within the classroom, the conversation may look like this:

'Please remember, Paul, that anything you search for on our iPads will be recorded and saved. I might check over the history on the iPads from time to time, too. I'm not doing this to be nosy, but because I care about your safety.'

Be sure too to remind your child that: **'If you ever spot something on the internet that makes you feel worried or uncomfortable, you need to share it with me. You won't be in trouble for any searches you have made. I just want to help you to use the internet safely.'**

I would also refrain from making out that the internet is exclusively a dark and dangerous place. When I start to discuss E-Safety with my students, they will often automatically remind me that it is dangerous; it is as if they have had this message given to them many times before.

'The internet is scary, strange things might pop up! Don't talk to anyone you don't know!'

Of course, is it good that the message seems to be sinking in, but I also like to try and remind my students of the amazing ways in which the internet, and social media in particular, can be used:

'Don't forget, there are great ways in which we can use this technology, too! We can connect with people from around the world, show our ideas to a large audience and find out information about almost anything we want to. The internet is an amazing thing – we just need to use it carefully and respectfully.'

A final and important note here would be to try not to compare your school's expectations, or chosen websites, with those your child's friends may be using. While teachers will almost always appreciate suggestions for new resources, some websites are expensive to buy for the whole school. There could be a reason why the school has decided to use something else. Try to make the most of the websites and resources the school has bought into. Furthermore, don't underestimate the power of social media when looking for exciting technology-based lesson ideas to try with your child. I get so many creative and inspiring ideas from other educators and parents online. Be sure to save screenshots of interesting ideas you spot while browsing, and encourage your child to do the same if they find something that inspires them.

Submitting work electronically

Your child's school will probably be asking you to submit their work electronically, possibly through photographs on an online system. Try to explore how this format may work ahead of time. There's nothing more frustrating than grappling with a new piece of software when you're trying to make effective use of the time you have available to teach your child. Watching a short online video tutorial may help to minimise this; some websites even offer free training guides specifically created for parents.

When asking your child to take a photograph of their work and upload it, resist the temptation to take the picture for them, even if it might save you a lot of time. The sooner your child builds mental and muscle memory associated with completing a task like this, the more independent they will be with managing their own work submission in the future. Once uploaded, ask your child to check over the work: can you read what is written? If not, start again. This excruciating process may leave you wanting to tear your hair out, but once the skill is learnt, it's one they will likely remember.

Reflection is appropriate once a child has uploaded a piece of work; make sure they're not just selecting the first thing they've found on opening their notebook.

'Why did you choose this piece of work?'

'What skills did you develop when completing this piece of work?'

And, 'Next time, how could you improve this?' are all questions you might want to encourage your child to answer when they type under or scrawl on top of their electronic work copy. My students also seem to want to add images, shapes and doodles on top of almost everything they decide to upload. Be realistic and balanced

with this process, and try to let them keep ownership of
their learning even at this stage.

Part II

—

Learning

5.

Lessons, skills and home projects

So you've done your prep and gathered your resources. What now? What will home learning look like? How do you actually do it?

As ever, before we get into specifics, here are some general principles to keep in mind.

Making learning memorable

You will almost certainly have tasks sent to you from school – some worksheets, for example – and you may have bought specific subject workbooks as well. How will you actually use these in your home?

As teachers, we are always trying to link our lessons with skills that are going to help our students in the future, and to make lessons feel as 'true to life' as we can. Although it is undeniably enjoyable and interesting to learn about, for example, Ancient Greece, at primary school age we prefer to focus more on the skills obtained through questioning, research and creation than we do on the recollection of facts, names and dates. This is why I would strongly encourage you to take a project-based approach to tasks that have been provided for you and your child. If you have been asked to learn about measurement, consider how this might be made more tangible for your child.

'I can see that today we have been asked to learn about measurement. I'm sure we can have fun with this task! Why don't we consider rearranging the furniture in your room? It has needed a change-around for some time now. Maybe we could measure the floor plan and see if there is a different place we could put some of the furniture?'

I understand this sounds a little bit 'out there' and arguably more effort than it's worth, but a project like this might be a good way for your child to develop their understanding in a memorable and practical way. If that sounds a bit too adventurous to start off with, there is nothing wrong with measuring the height of family members, pets or even the distance that a toy car can travel down a ramp. Work with the interests and suggestions of your child.

We try to encourage students to be problem-solvers within the classroom; I have in the past tasked my children with creating storage units to help keep their desks tidy, something they enjoyed planning, creating and evaluating. The units were pretty wonky, but my class felt ownership and pride in their creations. Yes, they were eventually recycled . . . but even months later, my students were using phrases such as '**How can we solve**

the problem?' without my prompts. Have a look around your house; what is a problem that could be solved? How can you get your child to take ownership of the tasks around them? Think big, and make sure they know you are truly invested in the project. Find a way to see enjoyment in this kind of unstructured, design-based activity. Unfortunately they will probably be able to tell if you're just pretending; children seem to have a natural intuition for figuring out your true motives. Try to enjoy the process of discovery, even if it might be frustrating when your vision of a lesson ends up going off at an unexpected tangent.

Real skills – developed through action

When I'm approaching a new challenge with my students, I often pause to ask them, **'Where do we see this being used in real life?'** A lot of the time, my students will struggle to make connections between the academic skills they're taught and how they can be applied to real-life challenges. It may be a wonderful opportunity for you to help strengthen those connections, and for your child to realise that 'subjects' are not just taught in school – the skills are transferable.

'Why do you think we are learning this?' is another question that seems to generate an interesting discussion, even though 'I don't know' is often the initial response. Dig deeper, open up the discussion and don't be afraid to offer examples. 'Ah, I see we are learning about push-and-pull forces as part of your science lesson today. Where might we see examples of this in the real world?' Begin to discuss how swings in the park provide an excellent example of this, as well as opening and closing cupboards around the home. Challenge your child to go and, camera in hand, find five examples of these forces around the house within a fifteen-minute time frame. Even if their class teacher has not asked for the learning to be recorded in this way, I'd bet anything that they would appreciate your student's efforts, regardless. Don't be afraid to share examples of your child's own projects and enquiry. Even if it might seem as though you're not always getting a response, I can promise you this kind of effort is greatly appreciated.

Child-led projects may look different depending on what you have access to as a family. If you have a garden or outside space available, I recommend using this as often as possible. Don't feel as though your maths time should always be spent in a certain space; it is perfectly acceptable to shift your environment, even if just for a change of scenery. I have been known to decide, last minute, without any prior thought, to shift my entire lesson outdoors in order to make the most of the warm afternoon sun and a cool breeze. Similarly, I have embraced the snowy weather and challenged my students to create the heaviest snowball they could in order to enhance an otherwise uninspiring lesson on units of weight. I distinctly remember our entire school cancelling curriculum-based learning for the afternoon to focus on a solar eclipse, a learning opportunity and real-world discussion that we just couldn't miss out on. Sometimes you have to learn to follow your gut feeling and adapt depending on the situation you are presented with.

'*I can't do it!*'

When a child struggles to grasp a concept or complete their work, don't panic! Struggle, confusion and problem-solving is quite healthy. It's normal for students to get stuck and, at times, frustrated. Problem-solving is an important skill that we want to encourage, rather than spoon-feeding the solutions to everything, never allowing for growth and the independent development of skills. Of course, if half an hour later there has still been no progress, it is important to intervene in the same way a teacher would.

'**Which part of this task are you finding difficult?**' or '**Where could we look for a solution?**' may be effective phrases to use. There is also a lot of power in splitting tasks, a strategy a project team might operate.

'**Perhaps if I look for some new ways to connect these sentences together, you could look for some interesting adjectives to describe the characters. Then, we can put our research together and build our story from there!**'

Even with the youngest children, the principle of making them feel you're both working on separate parts of something together can be very effective. This can be as simple as one of you listing the coloured pens you'll need for something and the other going to fetch them. This form of collaborative task delegation might be exactly the push your child needs to go on to work independently. If you are working with a younger child, who may not yet be constructing full sentences, you can always encourage them to follow your lead. Writing out letters and symbols for a child to copy may seem like too much of a simple solution, but a lot of early learning relies on mimicking skills and copying actions. Just think about all the songs and games we share with young children: they often include clapping, movement and call-and-response phrases, as this helps the learning to become more easily remembered.

Should I buy extra workbooks?

When I find myself on a sudden health kick, the first thing I tend to do is go online and buy smoothie recipe books, training guides and download organisers promising that I'll be able to hit my goals within a couple of months. It's tempting for any of us to whip out our debit or credit card and go online when we feel under pressure to solve a problem quickly. Don't feel guilty if this was one of the first steps you took when considering the difficult job of teaching your child from home; others will have done the exact same thing. I imagine many parents will have sat down with their child, opened up the first page of a maths study guide and declared, 'OK, page one, off we go,' only to be met with confusion by their child, who may not have been used to learning in this way. In this part of the book, I want to discuss workbooks: whether you should buy them, how they can be navigated effectively and how to link the contents of the guide with the curriculum expectations of your child's school.

Balancing schoolwork with additional lessons

For primary teachers, it can be difficult to balance the expectations of home learning and make the work suitable for each child. Even if you feel as though home learning expectations may be quite well balanced, there will always be some parents who want more tasks, and others who feel it is too much and want less. The end goal is always to develop your child's ability to complete tasks independently, while not ignoring how useful and effective collaboration can be, too. Start by taking a look at the work that has been provided by your child's class teacher. Share an open, honest discussion with your child.

'How do you feel about the tasks Mr Barrett has sent for you to complete today?'

'How long do you think it will take you to complete your spelling challenge today?'

It might also be interesting to ask:

'If we could find more information about this in a book, would you like to try some extra challenges?'

Try to empower your child, and give them the chance to identify which tasks may take them longer to complete. If they feel as though the option to complete extra challenges through the use of a study guide or workbook may be enjoyable and useful for them, embrace this. If they cringe away at the sight of the guide or begin to get increasingly frustrated at this sort of challenge, perhaps consider whether or not it will be worth the inevitable conflict.

Your child's class teacher will be working hard to ensure that the tasks sent home are age-appropriate and balanced and will revise them at the end of each week, adding more or less depending on the feedback provided by parents and by their school's senior leadership team. Trust yourself to the process and the work expectations that have been given you. If you want to offer feedback or suggestions, I believe most teachers would receive your ideas gratefully. In my experience, children begin to find comfort in the structure of a routine after a couple of weeks; and of course, they will have days where they are more or less motivated.

It's unlikely your child's class teacher will direct you to go and buy a specific workbook, but there's no harm in sending a quick message to them, asking if they have any books they would recommend that link with the schemes used within the school. For example, your child's school may be teaching reading through phonics, and may have paid for a specific scheme to teach this. If you buy a workbook that teaches through a different method, you and your child will potentially end up confused and frustrated. Try to make links between the content taught at the school and any additional resources you choose to buy.

Navigation of workbooks

If you've made the decision to buy some workbooks alongside the content provided by your child's class teacher, I think it's a good idea to learn how to navigate and make the most of this resource. We want to try and avoid confusion, frustration and burnout; children should feel empowered by the work we provide them with as they grow towards independence. As an example, let's consider a maths study guide you may have bought specifically designed for your child's age group. As your home learning may not be starting off from the beginning of the academic year, it probably doesn't make sense to open the workbook at page one, point at the page and say, 'Off we go.' First, I would recommend avoiding using the book chronologically, unless you're using it entirely separately from the work provided by your child's school. Teachers will cycle through maths units over the course of the year, revisiting different strands of the curriculum and teaching skills, making links and revising past content. If your child is currently focusing on shapes within their classwork, it might be confusing for them to open a workbook on a page that focuses on multiplication.

Try to use the book to extend their learning, rather than introduce new or unfamiliar topics.

If your child is unable to take in the content of a study guide independently, the work may be pitched at too difficult a level for them; if the work is completed in a matter of seconds, again the book is not suitable for their personal level. As the expectations of the curriculum are subject to change every couple of years, you may find that the content of a study guide ranges quite drastically depending on the year of publication, or the company that has produced the guide. Keep an open-ended discussion going with your child to figure out if the work has been pitched at an age-appropriate level.

'Does this look similar to some of the work you do when you are at school?'

'Have you seen questions like this before?'

'Do you think you could answer this question without my support?'

Build a picture of your child's understanding as you explore the guide. You can also create a guide of your own using minimal resources: a short story, poem or magazine article can be used to encourage your child to answer comprehension-style questions:

'Why do you think this poem was written?'

'Can you find some new words in this poem for us to learn more about?'

'Why do you think the character responded in such a kind way at the end?'

Even books with a few simple words can be used to generate mature discussions and very basic resources can be used creatively. Your child is most likely used to learning through being asked questions and working things out through picture and text clues.

6.

Core subjects – project ideas

Because there is such a massive range of learning to cover in primary school, I'm going to try to concentrate on the fundamentals of subject-specific projects. As we've discussed, they can be a great way of connecting what your child is learning to their growing experience of the real world.

In this section, I will share some practical, easy-to-resource ideas for a number of different home learning projects. Of course, I am not able to make assumptions based on the age of your child, the curriculum they are learning from and their prior experience, but I hope what you read here inspires you to generate some ideas of your own. Remember, this is only useful if you want to include additional learning opportunities; the classwork provided by your child's teacher should be sufficient without having to add further learning. Be guided by the enthusiasm of your child, the resources available to you and the time you have to try to incorporate these activities.

For maths, you might wish to look into practical activities involving shape and construction. Don't feel as though activities such as building or modifying construction blocks are only meant to be used with younger children; I have in the past used physical materials like this with much older students. Use construction as a chance to explore size, weight and quantity. You can ask children to create repeating patterns, arrangements that show symmetry and different systems for categorising the materials you have at your disposal. Sometimes it can be nice just to see what your child chooses to create, before asking them to explain their ideas. **'I see you have organised our blocks into size order – why did you choose to do this? Is there another way you could arrange them?'**

If you'd like to add further learning to any work that is being provided by your child's school, you may want to work alongside your child to think of some project-based learning that can take place in your home. As always, it's important to hear your child's thoughts, opinions and suggestions and to include them within the design process. To start out, check in with your child and find out what they are interested in. If that means linking some projects with video games, celebrity role models or pop culture, you may wish to consider doing this. It may feel strange at first, but particularly when children are younger, teachers know the value of meeting them at the point of their passion about something. When they are older, it's more likely children will be able to connect with projects that previously may have been less interesting to them, as they will have developed more research skills and will have a broader knowledge of how to investigate a new topic.

Try to balance your child's own suggestions with values you also consider to be important, such as family history, real-world events and practical skills. Once you have noted down some suggestions your child has made, you can begin to create projects that utilise their strengths and help to develop new skills.

'Remember when you designed that information booklet in school about the life cycle of a plant? You arranged it so creatively. It was so easy for me to understand the information. Why don't we use a booklet like that to record our research on mystery books? Let's build on a skill you are already confident with.'

Better still, have your child reach this conclusion by themselves by asking, **'Can you remember a time you presented your work in a way that made it easy for the person reading it to understand?'**

Try to develop an action plan – perhaps something like this:

- what is the key question that will drive the learning
- what you want to try and find out
- why it is important to conduct this research
- who might find it useful
- what the result of this project might look like

For younger students, I must mention the importance of repeating skills. For example, if your child has previously managed to fold paper to create a basic 'book' before adding illustrations inside, encourage them to repeat this task in order to reinforce it. You don't need to be applying entirely new and ambitious skills to each activity, every day. Repeating a skill can be key to remembering it.

Home projects: maths

Mathematics allows for the exploration of rules, logic and systems. Printing out or creating a blank grid to write ascending numbers in is an effective way of giving you lots of different task ideas, with minimal time spent creating a resource. Your child can then be encouraged to identify odd numbers, or multiples of a number, as well as counting forwards and backwards. These number grids are a solid resource that are often utilised in the classroom with all age groups.

You may also want to investigate more practical examples of maths, such as measuring out the ingredients to bake a cake, or using coloured blocks to create a bar chart. I have often taken my students outside to observe the traffic (from a safe distance, of course), recording the different types of vehicles that passed us by, as well as the different colours and sizes. Although you might not be able to conduct the same research, you could ask them to quantify how many times a certain word is used within a book chapter, or how many times they spot a certain character in their favourite short cartoon. Ask them for suggestions and try to take them on board when creating this kind of activity.

Some days you might want to take a small idea or suggestion your child has come up with and turn it into a large-scale, spontaneous project. For example, a conversation about a particularly rainy morning could be a brilliant chance to collect rain water in a cup or glass and introduce a project about units of measurement. If, on other days, you are struggling to think of ideas to get started, be sure to search online for the curriculum your child studies, as well as their age group, and read through some of the key statements that are used by their teacher to create activities. If your child expresses an interest in their personal timetable and the structure of their daily routine, using a timer to keep an eye on the length of a task may be useful for them. Calendars, diaries and shopping lists can always be used to reinforce that ordering is a skill that's useful in real life, as well as for solving problem-style questions in school. I often show my students my personal diary – hiding anything I believe is too personal – as a real-life example of ways in which people keep track of important times, dates and appointments. Perhaps now might be a good time to get your child to start recording their routine in a diary, too. Remember, mathematical skills are hiding within so many everyday activities. Perhaps your child could help you add up the online grocery shop, or work out how much a book of stamps will cost, based on the price of each stamp, and calculate the remaining amount (once you've stuck a stamp on Grandma's birthday card)? Or they could work out how many steps it takes to get to the park for half an hour's exercise, measure how long one pace is and then work out how far away the park is? You could use the same method to measure your back garden or living room and then discuss different terms, such as diameter, radius, length and width. You could then pull all of this together to make a plan on graph paper.

As we discussed earlier, make sure to go back over what you've done that day, helping them to understand how it fits into the larger projects you are working on.

Home projects: developing writing skills

Writing is a fundamental skill that is taught effectively in many different ways around the world. It would be difficult to summarise all the ways you could teach writing. For some older children, being able to sit down and write a story is a skill that might come quite naturally, but for others it could be tricky to narrow down their thoughts, or even create ideas to begin with. If you ask a child to write whatever they want to write, they will probably find the challenge too open-ended. If you ask a child to specifically describe a baby dragon, you stand a much better chance of getting a creative response. By narrowing down your request, you have provided a smaller scope of potential avenues for your child to utilise, and yet they will be able to draw from the vocabulary they have begun to acquire since starting school and learning how to describe.

When setting writing tasks, we must ensure we keep our requests balanced. Too much structure, and there's little opportunity for a child to express their creativity, but without a structure it might be difficult for our student to get started. For younger children, consider ways in which to make the act of writing more tactile. Activities that encourage letter formation such as writing in sand, arranging pasta into shapes or even scrawling on a mirror using a dry-wipe pen might be more appealing and engaging.

Let's imagine how this might work in a home learning environment: '**Today your teacher has asked you to write a story about a character that has found themselves walking through an enchanted forest. How exciting! Off you go.**'

On hearing this instruction, it's likely your child is trying to build a mental picture of what such a scene might look like. It's a complicated process. They remember forests; forests are often used in storybooks. They sort of remember what 'enchanted' means; it reminds them of fairy tales. They might need a moment to process this, to draw from their past learning, before they are able to tackle the task at hand.

Ask guiding questions to try and support your child: '**Are there any unfamiliar words here we might want to put a line underneath? Which words do you remember seeing before?**'

Ideally you are wanting to encourage your child to create a bank of keywords that will support them once they start writing freely. 'Can you think of any describing words that might be useful for us during this task? I see the word "enchanted" has been used. Can you think of any other words that might link with this?'

Make a note of any suggestions, even those that might not appear logical. If your child suggests 'chimney', try not to automatically assume they are confused. Ask them to explain their reasoning:

'Because in Hansel and Gretel they are in a forest and then they are stuck in the house and there is a fire in the chimney!'

There may be a link somewhere; be sure to investigate and show that you value each contribution.

Once your child has begun to record their responses to a writing task, referring to the keywords that have been placed close by for easy access, it's important to reinforce that checking over the words they've written is an essential skill, as well as reading aloud. Even if your child's class teacher has not requested to hear an audio version of their writing, it might be a nice idea to send one over. As a teacher, I am always surprised and impressed by small forms of action that show my students presenting their ideas creatively.

When checking over a child's writing, be cautious when making too many corrections. Teachers will very rarely correct every single spelling error or underline multiple mistakes; we normally check for the objective that is the focus of the particular task. For example, if your child has described an enchanted forest using some interesting adjectives (descriptive words) but they have misspelt the language they chose to use, I would generally praise the child regardless, stressing that ambitious vocabulary is preferable, even if those words might be difficult to spell.

Try to acknowledge mistakes but balance this appropriately with positive feedback. What has your child done that is effective? How have they responded to the specific task they've been given? On the other hand, if they've been asked to include an example of speech within their work, and instead they have written a description, it might be time to take a step back and check their understanding of the objective.

Teachers will often use success criteria, or a list of expectations, to assess writing. This can be developed alongside your child; it doesn't have to be something you direct. Gather an understanding of how they normally structure their writing in order to build a tick list of expectations:

'What do you think a really good paragraph of a story would include?'

'Well, stories normally have characters. You need to know what they look like. Maybe they will show where they live. Maybe they will talk to their friends and go on an adventure to look for something.'

Your child has established their success criteria; they just need help organising their knowledge. They are aware that a story usually has a) a main character, b) words to describe, c) conversations between two characters, and d) a narrative that will take the main character on an adventure. Using this agreed format, you can begin to write based on the agreement that you will try to include these objectives within the work. This may be an effective way to find out more about the teaching and learning that has taken place at school for your child, and to figure out ways to incorporate these skills within a home learning environment.

Home projects: developing reading skills

I am frequently asked by parents, '**How can I improve my child's writing?**' or '**How can I improve my child's understanding of maths?**' It might come as a surprise to hear that I often suggest reading is a fundamental skill that can help to develop knowledge in other areas of the primary curriculum. A child skilled at maths may be unable to verbalise their methods if they don't have access to the vocabulary needed to express what they want to say. A child's writing is also limited to the vocabulary they have previously been exposed to; they will often revert to language that has been obtained through reading.

Cultivating a positive experience around reading is, in my opinion, one of the most important steps we can take to give our children the best start we can in developing a love of reading.

Your child might prefer listening to a story – for example, the sharing of a book at bedtime. Other children may take to reading independently, preferring that to reading a book aloud with others. Some children may struggle at first to discover a love of reading, although it is important we help them explore different types of text in order to find something that will inspire them. Understandably some children do take longer than others to find a way to embrace reading as a skill. As always, I suggest you take time to communicate with your child in order to build a picture of reading with them.

When I try this with my students, I often ask them to complete a timeline of their own experience with reading. I might introduce this by saying:

'When I was little, I loved listening to my dad's stories. He once read me a fantasy book, *The Hobbit*, and I was so inspired. For a short time I stopped enjoying reading, but that was mostly because I found it difficult to understand the different sounds within sentences. After a while, I discovered some interesting non-fiction books about Ancient Egypt; I was inspired once again! As a teenager, I found I had less time to read books, as I was always trying to balance my reading time with studying. Now, as an adult, I always try to make time for exploring new stories when I go on a trip, or whenever I need to relax.'

I drew this out on a timeline, mapping out the peaks and troughs associated with the different stages of my reading journey. In order to learn more about my students, I asked them to describe their own personal journeys. I explained:

'Of course, your journey won't look the same as mine.

You are younger than me, and you haven't been reading for as long as I have! But your journey is important, as learning to read is not a simple, straightforward challenge. There will be highs and lows, and at times you will struggle. Together we will work to find out the best ways to help you stay inspired with reading.'

You may wish to help your child verbalise their experiences of reading, mapping it out like this on a timeline. If your child is younger, you might be discussing the early stages of reading, such as learning the sounds that make up words. You can still access this task: begin by discussing how it feels when someone reads you a story, and how it might be different when you are asked to identify the sounds within a word. Ask them what their future goals may be:

'I want to be able to read a whole book by myself!' or:

'I want to read a non-fiction book that links with our new science unit.'

By developing a sense of positivity around the reading journey, you can help your child to understand that it's an ongoing process, rather than a skill that is suddenly acquired.

WHY MUST IT ALWAYS BE UNICORNS?!

Parents will often confess in our meetings that they are worried about their child only enjoying a certain type of book, for example, comic books, or even a specific fixation, such as 'monster books'. They will say this is the only type of book their child reaches for or enjoys. In a perfect world, we want to give our children the best start we can with a broad, varied exposure to different text types. However, in reality we must accept that, just like us, they will have preferences they will reach for when given a choice. I often tell parents not to worry, and to allow their child to become immersed in whatever type of book they have gravitated towards; we are trying to build an unforced enjoyment of reading rather than make it feel like a challenge. Parents will also tell me that their child is obsessed with a certain author or book character; I generally tell them to embrace this stage. If your child is obsessed with unicorns, let them indulge in lots of books that are unicorn-related while they are inspired and reading for enjoyment.

As a love of reading starts to build, we can gradually introduce the child to books that are similar to their chosen text type, eventually moving them on to books that may push them out of their comfort zone and on to new discoveries.

When reading with your child, it is important to show an interest in the book they have selected, even when the book might not be particularly enthralling for you. In order to build a child's reading level up to a stage where they can access longer chapter books independently, early reading skills must be taught. If your child's school teaches reading through phonics, be sure to find out which scheme is being used. Different schemes will use different variations of sounds and actions; teaching the wrong scheme may confuse your child!

When a book has been selected for your child by their class teacher, they will have tried to choose one that will offer a balance of independent reading with an appropriate amount of struggle. If your child is finding every word on the page challenging to the point where they can't read through a sentence, the book may be pitched too high for them. If they are reading the book easily, without pausing to decode a single word, they may require a more difficult text. An important issue to keep in mind, though, is that being able to sound out a word correctly is not on its own a full understanding of a book.

Often a child is capable of reading a text without making mistakes, but they will be unable to articulate the events of the story or define the words they have read aloud. It may sometimes be necessary to keep reading books that seem too 'easy' for them to check for this aspect of their reading.

Be sure to check their listening and comprehension skills by asking both direct and open-ended questions about the text.

An example of a direct question might be:

'Can you find the word on this page that has been used to describe the frog?'

Whereas a more open-ended approach might look like this:

'Why do you think the princess decided to run away from her home?'

I like to keep a note of words my students have found

difficult as they read, ready to return to for a discussion after they finish reading the book. Rereading a text may also be useful, especially if they read it effortlessly the first time; challenge your child to work on their expression and character voices now they are familiar with a text. Balance the reading, taking turns to read a line each, if your child is reluctant to read the entire book independently. This way, you can model the use of character voices and pace for your child to follow. I also think that audiobooks can be used effectively to model use of intonation and expression. Don't feel as though it should always be your child reading; balance this with audiobooks and apps that will read the book aloud to your child. There are many different ways in which to access and enjoy a good story.

If you feel as though your child may have exhausted a particular text, you might want to encourage them to write a review or design a new front cover for the book. I often ask my students if they would recommend the book to someone else, and who they might choose and why. I also want my students to know that they don't have to enjoy every book they read; they can dislike characters, events and structures of certain books. I encourage them to justify their opinions, even at an early age, and use this to build a bank of knowledge that will symbolise the sort of book they might reach for in future.

Teaching reading, or even a love of reading, can be a difficult job for parents and teachers alike. Try to be kind to yourself during this process, to avoid ending up in conflict situations with your child. If you are picking up a book of your own and reading in front of your child, they may be more likely to see it as a positive activity that is used for enjoyment, not just because their teacher has told them they have to do it. Some days you may feel as though you are making a lot of progress, and other days as though you are taking a step backwards; just do the best you can when promoting a love of reading.

Home projects: science experiments

I have a secret love-hate relationship with science as a subject. The projects often take a long time to prepare, they don't always go to plan and the actual point behind the experiment may be missed out entirely based on the results gathered at the conclusion. That being said, when I am able to get it all working, my students always seem to enjoy learning through experiments and practical projects. For the purpose of scientific enquiry, please remember that an 'experiment' doesn't have to be a messy, hyper-resourced lesson, complete with lab coat and smoky chemicals. An experiment can be as simple as observing insects in the garden, or measuring the length of your shadow as it changes through the day. It doesn't have to be messy – thankfully! Generally you will find that most schools will use the word 'investigation', which sounds less intimidating than 'experiment' and a whole lot tidier.

Before launching into an investigation of any sort, be

sure to let your child know the importance of discussing

- what you want to know/find out
- what you are expecting will happen (making a prediction), and
- what you will need in order to conduct the investigation.

Perhaps your child's teacher has sent through an activity that links with changes in materials: if so, this might be a great opportunity for your child to conduct an investigation that involves freezing materials, or even combining ingredients to create something malleable – yes, I am unfortunately talking about making slime. Organising your project before starting is crucial, as it is at this stage that your child will be forced to imagine what might happen as a result of an action taking place. Recording their initial thoughts and ideas also means that a more mature form of reflection can take place at the end of the investigation:

Is this what we expected to find out?

Why do we think this happened?

How could we repeat this in the future in order to see if our results might change?

Be sure to open up a discussion with your child, rather than telling them what the investigation is they are going to be conducting, complete with resources readily arranged. We want our children to feel as though they are empowered by their research and in control of the decisions being made. Consider starting a discussion by finding out more about what they already know and what has been learnt in school:

'I noticed that your teacher Mr Watts sent you an online activity about plants this morning. Why do you think he sent this over?'

Hopefully your child will start to make a connection as to why this has been requested.

'We started learning about growing plants. Maybe he wants us to find out about how they grow.'

'Ah, I see. Do you think there might be a way for us to learn about plants from home?'

'Yes, let's grow some plants!'

Be sure to break up the process, explaining that you need to discuss the resources that must be gathered, as well as the steps you need to take to conduct an investigation involving growth:

- Are you looking for a certain size of plant, a certain colour, or number of leaves?
- How will this help you to gather information?
- What is the key question that will drive your investigation?

Although this might sound like a lot of extra work, I believe that children respond more positively to challenges when they have been involved in the creation process. If you are running short on ideas that link with specific areas of the curriculum, be sure to search online for videos, blog posts and tutorials. Or have your child conduct the research for you, in order to save you an extra job!

When planning exciting investigations, it's best to try and work with resources that are easily accessible to you and your family. Thankfully, Mother Nature often arranges this for us: consider how seasonal changes can provide exciting opportunities to find out more about the world around us. If you are lucky enough to have access to a garden, consider creating a space that is made for gathering materials that can be found over the course of the year. Leaves, feathers and even animal fur can generate a multitude of discussions with your child. Leaves will change in appearance, provoking conversations about seasonal change, habitats and the environment. Feathers are a great way in which to look at insulation and the mechanics of flight, and finally, discarded animal fur could be gathered and used to create a small nest for insects or birds, which at a later point can be observed and discussed. A bird feeder could be constructed from cardboard, or an upturned plant pot could be transformed into a hedgehog hotel.

As always, encourage your child to think creatively when investigating in this way, and consider recording the steps you have taken in a small project journal, complete with photographs (encourage your child to become an expert wildlife photographer, even if both of you have to use a lot of imagination to make this happen!).

7.

Additional subjects – project ideas

Each school will have a unique set of approaches to the way in which its subjects are taught, approaches that will include the expectations that have been set by the curriculum used. Again, it's always useful to check your school's curriculum before launching into home learning projects that relate to specific subjects, such as geography or history. Some schools may not teach these subjects independently, or may have other names for them entirely. A blend of skills may be taught under an umbrella title such as 'humanities', or 'the arts'. Depending on your child's age, it might not be something that has been introduced to them formally yet. Some schools may avoid naming individual subjects entirely, instead choosing to group lessons into skills, topics or themes. As always, keep a close eye on the work that has been sent home for your child to complete by their class teacher in order to build effectively on the skills that have already been taught.

Home projects: history and geography

As I've mentioned above, before introducing specific subject titles such as geography or history, be sure to check with your child's school curriculum for the correct names used for these subjects. Some schools may teach the subjects through a theme, such as 'exploration', gathering together many different skills and teaching them through a combination of lessons. In my opinion, when taught well, all of these subjects will blend seamlessly and develop multiple skills, and don't necessarily need to be taught as stand-alone subjects.

If you want your child to develop an interest in history, I would suggest starting locally before broadening their skills to include more global studies. For example, begin by building your child's sense of their own personal history, then go on to introduce them to the history of their home country and beyond. Taking an interest in your personal history can be a fun investigation for anyone; it might even be something you have wanted to look into for some time. Consider using this time as an opportunity to investigate your personal heritage alongside your child. Make predictions:

Do we think that all of our family members lived in this country?

Do we think some of our family members might have been doctors, or artists, or explorers?

Ask your child how they wish to conduct their research: interviewing family members, looking into heritage discovery websites, searching online for the history of their family name. We want our children to develop a sense of themselves before they go on to look into the historical discoveries of others.

You might wish to encourage your child to look at where they currently live before asking them to compare and contrast this with other places around the world. For example, you might want to open up a discussion with a question such as:

'Our home town, Sheffield, is famous for producing steel. I wonder what other cities are known for? How could we find out more?'

Perhaps you could look for photographs or film footage of the local high street in the past.

While it might be fun to teach specific time periods and discoveries to our children, such as Ancient Greece or Ancient Egypt, it might be more useful to look at the skills that can be developed through investigating multiple time periods, such as looking at 'discoveries', 'belief systems' or 'inventions'. This way, we can encourage our children to look at new information through a conceptual lens, rather than simply learning a list of facts that may not be as useful to them in the future. We want them to gain a broad range of knowledge that is relevant in more than one country, as our children may wish to travel and live elsewhere later on. It is important to show them that world history is interesting and that links can be found between the experiences and discoveries that different countries have made, rather than focus heavily on the specific facts related to a time period or place.

To summarise, try to develop an interest in history that builds from personal, to local, to world history, depending on the age of your child.

Although you may be able to make a lot of links between geography and history when opening up discussions with your child, I would encourage you to spend time learning about the culture and belief systems of different countries, as well as their geographical location. Gather resources such as an inflatable globe, an encyclopedia and various examples of maps in order to make the learning visual and appealing. If you have taken a trip in the past, consider collating some of the photographs from that trip. Discuss the meals you shared, what clothes the locals wore and places of interest you visited. Use this as an opportunity to reflect on positive past memories, as well as generate questions to help your child compare and contrast this experience with other countries.

'**Do you remember the time we saw flamenco dancers when we visited Spain? I wonder what sort of traditional clothing is worn during celebrations in other parts of the world. Maybe we can investigate this today.**'

Use any prior knowledge your child has to further their learning.

Scavenger hunts and orienteering are exciting ways in which to develop a range of different skills, such as map-reading, problem-solving and logic. If you are fortunate enough to have access to an outdoor space, consider mapping out the area with your child and have them hide or retrieve certain objects according to their coordinates. Better still, time this activity using a stopwatch in order to turn it into a game where the results can be quantified. Have fun using terminology such as travel, turn, North, South, East and West in order to help your child navigate an open space. If you don't have access to an outdoor space, you might wish to challenge your child to retrieve items from around your home that match certain criteria: something smooth, something made out of plastic, something that represents a different country. Create games and challenges alongside your child to keep them keen, active and involved with their own learning.

Creative expression and physical activity

When getting to know a group of students, I'm usually able to figure out quite quickly how they enjoy expressing themselves creatively. Children will often verbalise, or show you, that they have an interest in drawing or painting. By watching the way they respond to presentation or group work tasks, I am able to identify which children gravitate towards drama or performance as a form of communication. Children who enjoy physical activity or who take part in sports such as football, dance or gymnastics will talk fondly of their extracurricular activities with their peers. In order to build a picture of a child, and create learning opportunities that are fun, engaging and personalised, it is essential to find out what motivates and excites them. While it might feel like a home learning environment is more limited than a primary school, it could be the perfect time to allow your child to discover more about themselves creatively by developing new skills and uncovering new passions.

Home projects: art and design

Apologies in advance: it is going to get messy. And that's part of the fun. Some days, you might want to stick to your carefully cultivated home learning timetable; other days, you might want to go off at a complete tangent. Consider allowing your child the opportunity to have a full day consisting solely of creative projects. Drawing, painting and construction are all skills that are developed through play and creation at school. If possible, try to get your child to consider putting together a brief before embarking on a creative journey:

- Why are we making this?
- What materials might we need?
- What skills are we hoping to develop as a result of this task?

A design brief, such as creating packaging for a product or an animal mask for a performance, might help your child to understand that normally when we create, there is a reason behind the decisions we make. Unless they just want to splash paint haphazardly over a piece of paper. That can be fun, too.

For simple projects that require minimal resources to set up, consider printing an image for your child (for example, an animal's face), slicing it in half, sticking it onto paper and having them draw the other half of the image. You could challenge them to use a particular art style, such as pop art, cartoon-style drawing or watercolour painting. This can be a fun thing for them to research online. Or, if possible, link this to something that has been suggested by your child's school; even a skill they have practised in the past.

My students always seem to enjoy designing to a brief. I might print a thin, faint outline of the human form and have them design clothing that links in with our current theme or topic of study. Although it was quite specific to a topic that was being taught in school, my students really focused on a task that involved creating clothing for passengers on board the *Titanic*. It was a great way to link their knowledge of this historical event with their fine art skills, and I could feel a really strong engagement from my students as it was something they had researched, designed and had ultimate control over. From a teacher's perspective, it was a convenient way to link multiple subject skills together, something that is often considered a success within a lesson. Resources that you have made can be saved and used again in future to link with new topics, themes and ideas.

Home projects: drama and imaginative play

Although it might not be a specific subject taught by your child's primary school, there are so many ways to incorporate speaking, listening and movement-based skills as part of your child's learning. I try to encourage my students to present their ideas in front of an audience, as well as tune in to their own thoughts, feelings and emotions, as often as I can. One of the greatest tactics to use in this kind of learning environment is the skill of observation: guide your child, rather than enforce rules or a script. That being said, many children enjoy reading from a script or writing one that links with the topic, or story, being discussed. If your child enjoys making plays and performing them to you (their ever-enthusiastic, loyal audience member), try to encourage this, as it is such an amazing way for your child to work on their speaking and listening skills, as well as improve their overall confidence. If you have the resources available, allow them to use a video recording device; they can film a day in their life, a tutorial or 'how to' video, or even a nature documentary with their toy animals.

If your child is older, consider how using technology may link effectively with this, as stop-motion videos can be created by taking a series of photos on your tablet or phone and combining them to create what looks like video when you scroll through them. Often, I get my students to use sticky notes to tell a story, before recording it with narration, scene by scene, like a comic book.

Although time-consuming to make, you will hopefully see how proud your child will be when they have the opportunity to present a performance of something they have created to an audience, even if that audience might have to be a family member or classmate via email.

With very limited guidance, I once observed my students set up their own 'classroom' complete with a teacher, students and lesson resources. It was fascinating to watch as they established who would become the teacher, and how one of the girls started to select students to answer her questions, offering house points as rewards to the children willing to join in with her game. Listening to the way she spoke, I couldn't help but smile and think, *is this what I sound like when I teach?* Soon, almost two-thirds of the class had gravitated over to this imaginative role play area and were joining in, even delegating the role of head teacher, school receptionist and classroom assistant to children; everyone had a role. I did not set this up. I didn't intrude and acknowledge their activity, spoiling the magic surrounding it. Quietly, I passed a couple of items to children, such as pens, question cards and books, silently encouraging them to build educational items into the world they had created.

Sometimes, the best action is to observe and allow the students to create, rather than stepping into a director role. I must also add that this was not a task done with specifically younger children; older students actually enjoy being given the opportunity to play in this way too. Feel free to join in, especially if you're invited, but refrain from taking over entirely. Watch the magic unfold!

In the real world, I understand that a magical role-play-style environment is much harder to cultivate when you are alone with a single child, without the social interaction that makes this kind of activity so successful. It is much harder to replicate a bustling classroom environment when you can't share your ideas and communicate your thoughts to a group. In order to give your child an audience, you might want to consider filming their speeches, poetry recitals or story read-alouds with a specific viewer in mind:

'I know your cousin loves this author, too – perhaps we could read a chapter from his book and send it over to her. I think she would love to see your performance!'

Try to make a real-life connection, or purpose, for your child. Uploading their work to a sharing platform used by their school may also help to build a connection with the other students in their class. If your child is enthused by the thought of making props or visual resources to enhance a performance, try to encourage this, too. What might look like a cardboard box stuck on top of a toilet roll tube to you might be a perfect representation of a video camera to your child.

Have a go at seeing the world through their eyes, and get excited about the ideas they share with you – no matter how unusual and dramatic they might sound. If your child is more reserved and shy when presented with a speech-style activity, try not to worry. Some children take much longer than others to find this kind of confidence. I have personally taught many different children who started the year incredibly shy, only to leave the class at the end of the year full of confidence and drive. It might not happen immediately for your child, and that is OK; provide lots of opportunities for them to find their voice, no matter how quiet, and they will begin to build their confidence.

Home projects: physical education

Unless you have the ability to set up team games for your children, complete with apparatus, a scoring system and a trained referee, I would approach physical education with a very open mind. Put simply, find a way to get your child moving! Although in a perfect world there might be more structure for this, it's unlikely your home is set up in a way that offers a broad range of different sports opportunities for you or your child. There are many excellent online video tutorials that share dance routines, fitness challenges and even martial arts exercises for you and your child to follow along with. As always, be sure to gather ideas and work with feedback from your child. They might be able to recall warming up for fitness at school using stretches and breathing exercises; let them show you what they can remember. Take inspiration from their knowledge and movements.

Consider starting each day with around half an hour of body movement or mindful breathing. It might be a nice idea to save a bank of useful online resources and label them from Monday through to Friday; I have this set up on my school computer for mindful breathing videos to make sure the activities are fresh and do not start to feel repetitive. Although it might be hard to think outside the box when mixing up physical activity with academic learning, it is possible to make connections between the two. Consider practising times tables, or doubling numbers, while passing a ball back and forth outside. If you are able to, hide phonics sounds around the house and have your child race to make complete words using them.

When your child seems to be showing that they have reached their mental capacity for the day, have them 'reset' by following a yoga or dance routine online. It might provide just the mental stimulation they need in order to return to, and improve on, a difficult task. The creativity I have seen on the internet recently with ideas of ways in which to combine skills and subjects is astounding. If it sounds like a crazy idea, consider trying it anyway. You might find it's the key to keeping your child active, both physically and mentally.

Thinking back to my first year of teaching, I clearly remember an afternoon where my outdoor activity plans had been thwarted by the ever-unpredictable Manchester weather, and without the time to reach for a well-resourced backup plan, I was forced to think creatively in order to enthuse my class of thirty ten-year-olds. Grabbing an old duffel bag, I quickly stuffed it full of random items, probably consisting of a ball, a clipboard, a pen, an empty box, a shoelace, a roll of tape and a random piece of fruit. Hoping to spark an interest among my students, I challenged them to think of a game that could be played using all of these items. The game would need a scoring system, a set of rules and, ultimately, a way in which to win. Everything else was left up to them and their chosen teams.

This soon turned into one of the most active, compelling and inventive afternoons I ever spent with this particular class, and so was born an activity that I would keep up my sleeve for rainy days, class parties and even future job interviews. The Mystery Bag PE Lesson was a roaring success, and it didn't even require any planning time.

Taking inspiration from this short story (and happy memory) of mine, consider how, with the right amount of enthusiasm and energy, a random selection of items might be used to create an exciting activity.

8.

Mindfulness, well-being and work – life balance

How to tell when you both need a break

As a parent, you probably feel like you deserve a break before you even wake up in the morning. I agree – you need a break. You really do deserve one. I find nothing more stressful than having to layer more tasks on top of an already hectic schedule. It is highly likely you have found yourself in a difficult position where you are re-evaluating your work–life schedule and considering the best way to incorporate your own child's work into your daily routine. In this chapter, I want to look at how to achieve a positive work–life balance, as well as ways to open up about well-being and the importance of knowing when to take a break.

There are many ways in which a student will try to tell you they need a break. We would like to think they would be direct and their request well reasoned, such as, '**I need a break, I've worked really hard to take in all this new information this morning and honestly, my** mind could do with a minute to rest up and refresh.' But we all know that it isn't always easy for our children to communicate such feelings to us. Children may hint at needing a break: fidgeting, asking deliberately misleading questions, requesting snacks, toilet breaks or even fabricating headaches or stomach aches to throw us off the task at hand. I'm not saying that these excuses aren't sometimes valid; children may need a break based on these reasons from time to time. We have to decipher when the request is legitimate, and when it is a cleverly disguised distraction tactic.

I do find it a little confusing when parents tell me that their child refuses to concentrate at home because they are always hungry and requesting snacks. Most primary schools will have just one, short snack break mid-morning and then lunch around midday. Students very rarely have any other food on top of this. I do, of course, encourage them to stay hydrated and I never limit water breaks. To be fair to the children, I probably snack more myself when working from home as a result of the food being there, right in front of me. Including a break with a snack at a similar time to when your child would have a break in school could be an effective way to try and minimise distractions related to food cravings; you can remind your child that there's a break in their work schedule coming up.

On the other hand, if I ever notice that a child is looking lethargic or is not working to the best of their ability, I will always take it seriously. Normally, a quick discussion will lead me to discover that

- the child has not eaten breakfast on that particular day
- the child has a worry or concern on their mind
- the child is dehydrated
- the child is not getting enough sleep

As always, communication is key. Rather than asking leading questions such as:

'**Why are you struggling to concentrate – is it because you are hungry?**' try to go in with an open-ended question such as:

'**Is there something on your mind? Is there any reason why you might feel different today?**'

Be sure to follow up with something that acknowledges the concern and that also implies there is a way to resolve the issue, for example:

'**I understand you are feeling worried about moving into a new class next year. I bet it's difficult to concentrate with something so important like that on your mind. At the same time, I think your mind will feel much clearer and more refreshed if you work hard to learn some new information today. You normally feel better when you achieve your goals! Shall we work together and take one more look at that science project?**'

Mindful breathing and relaxation

There is something a little bit unnatural about a silent classroom. I find it very unusual when my students do decide to work quietly on a project, or during a test. It feels much more productive when there's a buzz in the air, ideas being exchanged and the hushed, enthusiastic chatter of students asking questions and sharing their ideas. That's when I feel most comfortable as an educator; I can be the facilitator of learning, rather than 'in charge'. Recently I have been trying to incorporate more mindful breathing and relaxation into my class's daily routine. At first, it did feel quite uncomfortable. After working to create a routine, I can now say that it's something that helps both my students and myself to relax and clear our minds before taking on a new task or challenge. When setting up for some mindful activities with your child, I suggest gathering their input, rather than telling them, 'We are going to meditate every day before we do your spellings.' Ask what might be effective, making notes as you discuss:

'What helps you to feel calm?'

'If you are trying to focus on your work in a busy classroom, how might you do that?'

Discuss how some people might use music, lights or movement in order to achieve a sense of calm. There is a chance your child might have been exposed to some of these strategies at school, and perhaps you've never thought to ask them about this before now. If your child makes a suggestion you think is appropriate, see if there is a way to incorporate this within your home learning schedule.

In the past, I have entertained all sorts of interesting ideas for mindfulness. One child suggested that folding paper and following an origami tutorial helped him feel more focused. You know what? He was completely right. It did help him; it also helped some of the other students, too! If your child has not been shown this kind of mindful routine, consider searching online where you will find articles, videos and blog posts discussing the value of mindful breathing for younger children. I often use children's guided meditation or yoga videos that I've found online; these are all saved as shortcuts on my desktop for easy access. At first I found the non-verbal calm of the room to be uncomfortable; I had to embrace it myself in order to pass on this skill to my students. They might want you to join in with this, and honestly, it might be just as beneficial for you to take a mindful moment as it is for your child. Some days, it's exactly what we need to refresh ourselves as we work our way through a project.

Expecting, managing and reducing conflict situations

At some point during this unusual process, the inevitable will happen. There will be disagreements and periods of frustration for both you and your child. If we accept this with a positive mindset, perhaps it will end up being less upsetting for all involved. In the classroom environment, some days children will walk in and show signs that they are not feeling compliant, for whatever reason. Despite showering them with positivity and providing them with as many enriching learning opportunities as you can physically manage, there is a chance they will just not feel like connecting or engaging, and this may result in feelings of frustration for you and them. On days like these, my thoughts might run as follows:

'Why is she deliberately disrupting this lesson, does she not realise it took me over an hour to collate these activity booklets for her group?'

'Why is he purposely messing up our reading corner, when he saw how hard we worked on ordering the books into topics last Friday?'

Even after sharing a discussion and working to unpick a child's intentions, sometimes it is appropriate to admit that there are times when children will feel less engaged and will push boundaries to the limit.

Disagreements may be identified as lower-level responses, such as answering back, refusing to complete an activity or deliberately giving incorrect responses to see if it might start an argument. If a child reaches a point where a disagreement has escalated to tears, shouting or a physical response, I would refrain from trying to reason with them and take a step back. While this is not a book about parenting or behaviour management, it's fair to assume that if a child is in a negative mind space, it is not an appropriate time to start reminding them to stick to the timetable or focus on a difficult calculation. I have used many different methods of behaviour management in the past in a classroom setting, and I have no doubt that the structure outside of the classroom is an entirely different world; each family will have their own rules, expectations and ways of dealing with conflict.

Once a child has taken time to clear their mind, whether through time spent in a different environment, or just by having some time to themselves, you will need to reflect and try to look at the bigger picture. Be sure to discuss the situation openly and check that your child is still able to see things from your perspective, too:

'I'm sorry we had a disagreement earlier. I understand that you felt frustrated. I could tell you were frustrated when you got the answer wrong on your maths paper – it can be difficult when you work hard on something and the result isn't the one you were expecting.'

Show that you can identify the turning point or moment that caused the conflict. Reference it so as to highlight it as a trigger:

'I also think it's great we've got the opportunity to try this again, now we are both calm. I think you've made the right choice, and I'm proud of you for that.'

It's important, too, to give your child a chance to identify what might have happened:

'Why did you find that task so difficult?'

'How did you know that you needed a break?'

'What should we do next time we feel frustrated, to try and have this happen less?'

Reinforce that this is normal and that people will feel frustrated when they are having to work on new projects. Try to avoid promising that it won't happen again, or that expressing our feelings of frustration is not valid. Everyone has a different coping mechanism for such an event; your child is trying to figure out how that might look for them.

9.

Discussion and positive socialisation

Positive communication: creating a safe place for discussion

While you are educating your child in a homeschooling environment, whether that's by choice or as a result of world events, you should expect that they will have abstract questions that deserve to be acknowledged. While each family may have different agreed responses to such questions, I believe it's important to encourage your child to become a global citizen, and to challenge them to find out more about the world around them. Never underestimate a child's ability to connect with real-world issues and complications when they are given a safe place in which to question, research and discover.

In the classroom, I try always to answer my students' questions honestly in every situation where this is appropriate. If I feel as though something may be too mature for their age, or perhaps it would involve me divulging too much private information of my own, I might explain that a certain topic is not appropriate for discussion. I reflect on the best way to provide information to my students about sensitive subjects, especially when I feel as though they might find out information from other less dependable sources, such as through the media or from friends who may pass on misinformation in the playground. Playground discussions are all too often the result of an accidental internet search, or based on what a child has heard from an older sibling. I would rather my students come to me for more reliable information, even if it means approaching difficult discussion topics from time to time.

If you feel as though your child might not always trust you with information that may be worrying them, try to create a safe sharing environment in which they will not be reprimanded for how they acquired this information. In the past, I have heard of families setting aside thirty minutes of discussion time each week where nothing said during that 'safe' discussion will lead to anyone in the family getting outwardly angry, ideally generating a safe place for children to divulge information that's on their mind. While this is harder to set up in a school environment (schools often have a shared, whole-school behaviour policy), it might be a useful approach for a parent to use when looking to build a sense of trust with their children.

A conversation that springs to mind is one I have had with seven-year-old students in the past:

'Why did you miss our art lesson on Monday, Ms Tollitt?'

'I did miss our lesson, didn't I! I had to go and get some information from my doctor. Remember a couple of weeks ago when I had a bandage on my wrist? I had to have an X-ray to check that nothing had been damaged. I'm sorry it meant that I had to miss your lesson.'

'Oh, OK. Will your hand get better?'

'Well, it seems like none of the bones are broken, which is good news. Of course, it might still take some time to completely heal.'

'That's good. My friend broke her leg once. It got better quickly, though!'

'Thank you for sharing. If you ever want to talk about this again with me, just let me know and we can have another chat.'

Of course, in this situation I could have simply told my student that I missed their art class because I was in a meeting. Perhaps that would have been a much simpler, less complicated response. Often we are tempted to give children answers that are easier to process, to avoid them going off at a tangent and asking too many personal questions. I firmly believe that my students deserve a version of the truth as often as I am able to provide them with one. Of course, if my students had been younger, I might not have gone into as much detail, especially to avoid causing them worry. Each situation is judged as a unique discussion that must be dealt with maturely and responsibly. But don't forget that part of learning is going to new places and finding out new things. The same idea applies at home as it does at school; don't be afraid of questions that take you and your family somewhere new.

Answering difficult questions

In the classroom, my students ask many questions every day. Many, many questions. I have no doubt that in a home learning environment too they will ask a lot of questions, if not more than they do at school, simply as a result of spending more one-to-one time with an adult. In the past, I remember feeling anxious when my students asked me questions about areas of the curriculum for which I had no answers. I used to try my hardest to give them some sort of response, even if it was unclear, or even incorrect. I am now much more likely to respond with:

'I'm actually not too sure about that one. What an interesting question. Perhaps we can investigate this together to find out more.'

This way, a question may lead to a discussion, involving research. If your child asks a question that seems very unrelated to the task at hand, for example asking about a political world leader while completing a spelling test, you might want to assume your child has heard or seen something, perhaps online, that has been on their mind for some time before they have chosen to ask the question. If you feel as though answering the question may lead to further questions and distract you from the challenge you are trying to complete, try to acknowledge the question rather than disregarding it:

'What an interesting question. Maybe we could discuss this later on, while we have our mid-morning snack. Let me write your question down now so we don't forget to go back to it!'

I have used this method many times in the classroom to show my students that I value their contributions, as random as they may seem, and will make time to go back to them at a more appropriate time. Usually this is enough for my students; they understand that I have listened to their question, and, rather than disregarding it, I have stored it away safely for further discussion later on. It may seem as though these random questions come in waves, especially when your child might in fact be trying to create a diversion; perhaps they are not too inspired by the academic task in front of them.

As adults, it is likely we procrastinate in similar ways, so we can't be too frustrated when our children try to do this too. I try to have similar expectations for my students as I do for myself:

Would *I* find this interesting?

How would *I* complete a task that I am less inspired by?

We all have deadlines to meet, not all of them appealing ones. We manage our own distractions every day, and it is necessary to communicate this clearly to our children so they begin to understand that working hard is a choice we make in order to receive positive results. Consider what works well for you. If you are also working from home at the moment, share an example of your work timetable, or how you're planning to arrange your time. Creating a sense of shared goals and achievements may help everyone to feel more motivated. You could always challenge your child to meet a target, while you work on a specific target of your own. Meeting together once you've completed your task may be a positive way to share an achievement – perhaps you could ask your child to decide if you have met your own target, too!

Bringing it all together

As a light-hearted way to conclude this guide, I wanted to try and imagine what a typical day might look like for you and your child while learning from home. Of course, some may argue that there is no such thing as a 'typical' day, when each family is equipped with vastly different environments, structures and available resources. In spite of that, I thought it might be interesting to try and imagine a couple of different daily structures and how an average day might materialise. Please remember, your child's teachers do not expect you to recreate the primary classroom. We do not expect top-quality learning to be taking place every minute of every day. It's a struggle for us to achieve this, too, even as teachers, with all the experience we have of working in education. We need to show our children that we care deeply about them and want to support them, giving them the best chance possible to achieve their dreams.

Let's imagine, for the sake of this scenario, that you have two children who are going to be taught using a home learning environment. Many families are choosing to start their day with exercise – what better way to get your child's brain active! In school, they might get this stimulation through running around the playground, or excitedly chatting to friends as they make their way to the classroom. Give them a chance to get active and become alert! After eating breakfast, you might want to meet with your child, or children, to take a look over the agreements that have been made. Set some goals alongside your child; you might want to get something practical sorted today from your own work schedule.

Vocalise that, and consider noting it down. '**This morning, I will write an email ready to send out to the people who work in my department. I'll feel great when it's finally done!**'

Hopefully your child will be able to identify a goal of their own: '**This morning I will finish the spellings Ms Beckett sent over to me, and I will also start my mystery story.**'

Check over your timetable for the day, identifying what might be the best way to organise your child's learning. Now is the time to discuss which challenges will be completed independently, and where you might be needed to step in, teach and support. Be sure to check over any slides, emails or announcements that may have been sent to you from your child's teacher; if any online video lessons are being used, make a note of the times for these, too. You might want to agree on and vocalise the expectations you have for your child, and arrange a time at which to meet and discuss progress:

'**I'm happy that you've identified your mystery story writing as a goal you have for today – you've got a good** memory! After you've written the first chapter, we can look over it together. Remember, Ms Beckett asked you to include some speech in your story. Can you remember how to use speech marks?'

A quick revision session may be useful in order to remind students of their prior learning.

Once a plan of action has been agreed, give your child the opportunity to complete some of their work independently. Even very young students are given plenty of chances to work without adult support in the primary classroom, using resources and prompts to help them stay on track when they get stuck. You might want to check up sooner, but a mid-morning snack time is a great opportunity for you to connect with your child and see how they have progressed with their schedule. If your child is much younger, of course they may require more one-to-one support, especially when learning phonics or early calculation.

Before going back to completing their work, I suggest taking a mindful moment with your child to relax and reset. You might want to tick some of the tasks off your to-do list at the same time as your child to show that you are both making progress, before taking on something else. A break that includes physical exercise, or a mental break (watch your favourite television show or YouTube channel) for a short time is perfectly acceptable. Returning to work is always going to be a little bit difficult, as it can be for us as adults. Positively reinforce the action of returning to a difficult task:

'Well done for getting back into your learning so quickly today – I think we can go over some of your calculations together now!' Often, if I make a big, positive fuss over a child who has made a smart decision, they will remember to do it again the next day. Or they might not; children are very unpredictable, as I am sure you know!

After your child begins to show signs of wearying or disconnecting from the tasks presented to them, you might want to introduce some more practical activities, such as the examples provided in Chapters 6 and 7 (project ideas) of this guide. Don't feel as though this drop in energy, or indeed a spike in testing behaviour, is due entirely to your child being deliberately difficult. Most teachers would agree that afternoon periods are much harder to teach, as the majority of children respond in this way. There's a reason why teachers usually try to arrange lesson observations during the morning – children will naturally be less focused, potentially more disruptive or more fatigued during the afternoon. Keep your activities student-led, practical, physical and engaging in order to try to maintain some focus.

If a lesson you've worked hard to create for your child appears to flop, please don't take this to heart. It has happened to me, and I am sure many other teachers, more times that I could possibly write about. Often we have an idea in our heads of how something will be received, and feel frustrated when we are unable to make that idea a reality; and sometimes lessons we think up on the spot end up getting the best-ever response from our students.

To conclude a day of homeschooling, it might be nice to spend a short period of time reflecting on the learning that has taken place. Ask guiding questions such as:

'What did you enjoy about your science work today?'

(Remember, try not to ask questions that are too vast. Make questions more specific.) It might be nice, too, to dedicate part of your routine to thanking one another, and discussing something that you're collectively grateful for as a family. This may need to be heavily modelled at the start, so share lots of examples to give your child ideas of their own.

'I really enjoyed seeing how you solved those addition questions this morning. It made me proud to think that you've listened carefully in school and that you can remember how to use these methods.'

Or even something as simple as:

'I really enjoy spending time with you and finding out more about your interests. You've made me very proud today.'

It might take a while, but the more your child hears specific examples of positive praise, the more likely they are to start using similar phrases to reflect on their own achievements.

Final thoughts

Teaching your child at home is an immense challenge. Anyone who thinks differently is in for a surprise. Every primary school teacher has had lessons where they've felt prepped up to the eyeballs and it still just hasn't clicked; the message has not been received. You finish the day with paint in your hair, glue on the carpet, desperately asking yourself, 'How many days till the weekend?' While teaching from home, the road will be full of bumps – it might feel like there are more bumps than road at first – but you'll get there, and you'll get there together with your child.

For me, teaching is so rewarding because of overcoming these challenges. When one of my students writes me a thank you note, or I see the look on her face when she sounds a word out by herself for the first time, I am always filled with pride and joy. When you are there to watch a child realise the world is bigger, richer and full of more amazing things than they ever imagined, there is no greater privilege, no greater joy. I hope this book helps you find some of those moments.

Never underestimate the simple, yet important, lessons children are learning through being around us, too; how to sew on a button, pot a plant or operate a washing machine. Here is an amazing opportunity for us to pass on practical skills, some of which are not able to be taught in a primary school setting. They'll learn so much from joining you, their role model, as you navigate your daily life.

If it ever feels as though you aren't getting positive feedback from your child, or they're reluctant to get involved with a range of different projects, remember that younger children may find it difficult to express feelings of appreciation towards those who are working hard to support them. As they grow, they may discover new ways in which to symbolise 'thank you'. You are not alone. There are millions of people going through exactly what you are. Try to find people you can talk to honestly about how learning at home is going, whether that's a family member, a partner or a friend. It may surprise you to realise what you and your child have accomplished together.

You've got this, I promise.

Katie Tollitt, April 2020

Websites, apps and recommended online resources

Listed here is a selection of websites, apps and online tools that may be useful for you when setting up a home learning environment. Some of these resources might have paid options that you may wish to invest in, but almost all will offer a free version, or a basic plan, that can be accessed without a subscription. I recommend saving these links in files on your computer desktop for easy navigation. As always, I would suggest checking with your child's school before paying to use any specific websites, and consider making effective use of the resources that the school has chosen to buy in to.

English

www.StoryBoardThat.com

Make simple, comic-book-style storyboards that can be saved, shared and emailed digitally. Great for recreating a story, or for exploring character traits. Choose a backdrop, add text and resize images to make your comic book creation completely unique.

www.LiteracyShed.com

Child-friendly videos that can be used to spark discussions, or that can be watched simply for enjoyment. Most videos have activity ideas to accompany them, which is useful for a quick-fire language lesson.

www.ReadTheory.org

Comprehension-style questions related to books, with tests available to check for understanding. Quizzes will make the challenges seem more interactive, personalised and hopefully enjoyable for your child.

www.SpellingCity.com

Create your own spelling lists, before practising them through a range of different interactive games. The cartoon-style animation used makes recalling spelling rules slightly more engaging for younger users.

www.TeachYourMonsterToRead.com

An award-winning website that encourages children to raise a virtual pet, while exploring letters, sounds and moving towards reading full sentences. Highly recommended by many educators, this can be a motivating and exciting online resource for younger readers.

www.GetEpic.com

More than 40,000 online books, quizzes and videos that have been categorised into reading genres, as well as sorted into age ability levels. Children can search for their favourite titles, as well as explore and discover new favourite authors. An invaluable classroom resource that I believe would be useful as part of a home learning setting too.

Mathematics

Search – 'Splat Square' (various websites)

Remember we discussed how number grids can be used effectively to practise a range of different mathematical skills? Splat Square is a great way to have children respond to questions, complete with a satisfying 'splat' sound that will amuse them (for a while, at least).

www.SolveMoji.com

Quickly generate calculations where the numbers have been replaced with cartoon images. A great quick-fire way to start a new lesson or mathematical discussion. The difficulty can be changed to suit the user, or randomised for daily challenges.

www.Nrich.Maths.org

Mathematical problem-solving ideas collated into easy-to-navigate categories that will suit the age of your child, as well as the resources that are available to you. They have recently added a section specific to home learning on their website, which focuses on independent problem-solving.

www.Transum.Org

Transum hosts a range of features including activities, puzzles and visual aids used to encourage mathematical investigation. My students particularly enjoy the games that relate to the learning of times tables, such as Tables Dash. Activities are arranged into daily challenges.

www.MathPlayground.com

Interactive online number games that are arranged carefully into grade levels, as well as into topics, such as animals, robots or sports, in order to enthuse children with a particular interest. Games with scores may also encourage children to beat their personal best.

Additional subjects

www.Kahoot.com – All subjects!

A popular website/app that allows the user to create their own quiz with multiple choice answers. With so many example quizzes available to access, it is a fun and interactive way to introduce a new topic, or consolidate skills that have been learnt.

www.Tynker.com – Computer Science

An incredible resource that promotes early computer science skills and coding for your child. Lessons can be accessed by all primary ages. I suggest starting with the most basic tutorial, as the difficulty soon creeps up. Coding is a great skill that you can learn alongside your child.

www.Newsela.com – Topic-based reading resource

Use Newsela to stay up to date with reliable news articles from around the world, pitched at a range of levels that can be changed to suit the age/ability of your child. Great for researching a new theme or topic and developing reading comprehension skills.

www.GoNoodle.com – Physical Education, Mindfulness

With over 100 free videos focusing on movement, mindfulness and improving physical well-being, GoNoodle is an excellent resource for encouraging children to get active. Use in short bursts between academic learning to refresh and re-energise.

www.kids.nationalgeographic.com – Geography

My students always enjoy the personality quizzes – especially those that link with endangered animals. Another personal favourite game is Animal Jam, which is a virtual world app where you learn about and care for endangered animal species. I highly recommend this one.

www.google.com/earth/ – Geography, History

Although your child will probably want to zoom in on their own house initially, Google Earth has the potential to virtually transport you to anywhere in the world, instantly. My students especially love the 'I'm feeling lucky' option, which takes you to a randomised location.

www.ReadWriteThink.org – History

This website can be used for a range of different subjects, however, I particularly like using the 'timeline' creator feature. Search for this on the main page of the website. The timeline is easy to navigate, with adding images, titles and text as a customisable design feature.

www.iNaturalist.org – Science, Geography

Found an unusual bug or plant in your garden? Snap a photo and upload it to iNaturalist online or via the child-friendly app. Find out more about the creature, as well as explore scientific findings in your local area.

www.BrainPop.com – Science

A fantastic website, featuring a range of inspiring project ideas. I would specifically recommend the science activities, as they are broken into categories such as space, forces and scientific enquiry. Sign up with your email to access some of their free interactive resources.

www.artlesson.blog/author/chrisgadbury – Art and Design

A personal teacher friend of mine, Chris Gadbury, has uploaded a wealth of invaluable art lesson resources to his online blog. Children can explore mark-making, patterns and even fashion design by watching his child-focused videos and step-by-step guides.

www.Crayola.com/education – Art and Design

Lesson plans and teaching resources are available on the Crayola website, some of which incorporate additional subjects as part of an art lesson. Look out for the '52 creative ideas for home learning' handout, which summarises a great selection of home learning project ideas.

www.MusiQuest.com – Music

Admittedly, I enjoy this one as much as my students do. Create simple melodies, songs and easily download them to share with friends and family. Enjoy learning about different music genres, instruments and composition.

Routine, organisation and printables

www.ClassDojo.com

A classroom management tool used effectively by many teachers around the world, ClassDojo allows you to give points to a character of your choice, as well as choose ways in which points are earned. Great for children who like to collect, or who like to track evidence of their achievements.

www.ClassroomScreen.com

Used by teachers around the world to organise information together on a computer desktop; I'm sure families will also find it useful! Timers, websites, videos and links can be collected here for easy future access.

www.TES.com

In the past, the TES website was released in print format. These days, it is used as an online resource-sharing hub for teachers all around the world. Although this might be used more often by your child's class teacher, you might find some of the lesson ideas and resources to be useful for home learning too.

www.twinkl.com

A useful resource hub for teachers that has recently added a huge selection of age-appropriate home learning resources that can be personalised and downloaded for use with your child. Additionally, many of the resources are available in different languages.

www.edu-box.co.uk

If you are looking to invest in some high-quality teaching and learning products, Edubox have keyfobs available to purchase. My personal recommendations include their phonics keyfob, which features flashcards of letters and sounds, as well as the curriculum overview keyfob, which shares the learning objectives for each year group. Based on the UK national curriculum.

www.Seesaw.com

Usually used in collaboration with your child's school, Seesaw is a website/app where students are encouraged to upload photographs, text documents and voice clips of their work in order to keep it saved in an online portfolio. Seesaw is user-friendly and has many helpful features, including assignments (pre-created) and online tutorials.

www.Padlet.com

A 'Padlet' is a type of online noticeboard, where you can pin ideas, images and notes. Multiple students and adults can collaborate on a document (if you allow this in the settings), which can be great for group project work.

Well-being and mindfulness

www.KidzBop.com – Dance

Enjoy the freedom of a pop-music party with your child, without worrying that inappropriate images or lyrics might accidently appear mid-dance. A child-friendly, welcome addition to any classroom or home learning celebration.

www.CosmicKids.com – Yoga, Meditation

Find your zen through guided relaxation, meditation and basic yoga routines. Use this alongside your child to practise finding moments of calm between lessons; you both deserve to take a mindful moment!

www.HeadSpace.com/meditation/kids – Meditation

Organised into categories that incorporate Calm, Focus, Kindness, Sleep and Wake Up, HeadSpace aims to make meditation simple and accessible for young children. Make use of their short video guides, calming music and step-by-step tutorials.

www.SafetyNetKids.org.uk – E-Safety

A very basic, easy-to-navigate introduction to staying safe online. Featuring information such as how to protect your online information and the early warning signs that suggest something may be unsafe, this website could be used to support an E-Safety discussion with your child.

Search 'Class Dojo Big Ideas' – Development Skills

Class Dojo isn't just used for classroom management, there are also some wonderful video resources and lesson ideas available on the Class Dojo 'ideas' page. Featuring important development skills such as growth mindset, gratitude, empathy and mindfulness, these videos can be used to spark an interesting discussion. I highly recommend this resource.

Acknowledgements

There are a lot of people who have played a role in helping me to become the person, and the educator, that I am today. I want to thank my family, for always encouraging me to create and question. Growing up in the Tollitt household, no project was deemed too unrealistic; we have always worked together to make our visions become reality. Thank you for teaching me how to construct, to design and to care for others. The skills I teach to my students today are a direct reflection of the upbringing I was lucky enough to experience.

Thank you to my close friends for helping me to keep an open mind when navigating the ever-changing world around us. I couldn't share my experiences of travel, adventure and resilience with my students if we didn't have an abundance of memories ready for me to weave into stories. Additionally, I am grateful to the friends who have been a key part of my time spent living in Hong Kong; thank you for making this country feel like a second home, and to those who have travelled across the world to visit me here.

To my partner, Neil, I appreciate your willingness to

get involved with my projects and the endless support you have given me over the years we have spent together. When we first met, neither of us had visions of living abroad, sharing our hobbies or the many adventures that life would take us on. Thank you for all that you do for me every day.

As a message for my students and colleagues, past and present: thank you for inspiring me to dream big. Every child and each family that I have had the opportunity to work alongside has made an impact on me as an educator. My practice has improved as a result of your action. Student-designed projects have challenged me to think creatively, and outside the box. I hope that the happy memories we shared will be remembered by you as you grow and shape your own futures.

Finally, to the reader of this book, I hope that its contents have helped to create meaningful and enjoyable learning moments between you and your child. Thank you for choosing to support me, and for trusting in my ideas.